Series/Number 07-132

LOGISTIC REGRESSION
A Primer

FRED C. PAMPEL
University of Colorado, Boulder

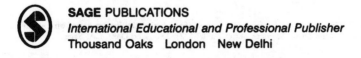

SAGE PUBLICATIONS
International Educational and Professional Publisher
Thousand Oaks   London   New Delhi

For information:

Sage Publications, Inc.
2455 Teller Road
Thousand Oaks, California 91320
E-mail: order@sagepub.com

Sage Publications Ltd.
6 Bonhill Street
London EC2A 4PU
United Kingdom

Sage Publications India Pvt. Ltd.
M-32 Market
Greater Kailash I
New Delhi 110 048 India

Printed in the United States of America

Library of Congress Cataloging-in-Publication Data

Pampel, Fred C.
    Logistic regression: A primer / by Fred C. Pampel
    p.   cm. — (Sage university pagers series. Quantitative
    applications in the social sciences; 07-132)
    Includes bibliographical references.
    ISBN 978-0-7619-2010-6 (acid-free paper)
    1. Logistic regression analysis; no. 07-132.
       I. Title.   II. Sage University papers series. Quantitative applications
    in the social sciences.
       HA31.3.P36   2000
       519.5'36—dc21   00-008060

This book is printed on acid-free paper.

14 15 16 17 18   14 13 12

Acquiring Editor:	C. Deborah Laughton
Editorial Assistant:	Eileen Carr
Production Editor:	Diana E. Axelsen
Production Assistant:	Victoria Cheng
Typesetter:	Technical Typesetting Inc.

When citing a university paper, please use the proper form. Remember to cite the Sage University Paper series title and include paper number. One of the following formats can be adapted (depending on the style manual used):

(1) Pampel, F. C. (2000). *Logistic Regression: A Primer.* Sage University Papers Series on Quantitative Applications in the Social Sciences, 07-132. Thousand Oaks, CA: Sage.

OR

(2) Pampel, F. C. (2000). *Logistic Regression: A Primer.* (Sage University Papers Series on Quantitative Applications in the Social Sciences, series no. 07-132). Thousand Oaks, CA: Sage.

CONTENTS

SERIES EDITOR'S INTRODUCTION

Logistic regression has pretty much come to replace ordinary least squares (OLS) regression as the data analytic tool of choice when the equation to be estimated has a dichotomous dependent variable. Even beginners know that OLS is simply "not done," or at least not published, when Y is binary. This advance in methodological practice has come about partly as the result of a steady flow, over the last 20 years or so, of instructive papers and books. Our series has made a major contribution to this educational effort, starting with the monograph, *Linear Probability, Logit, and Probit Models* (Aldrich and Nelson, No. 45). Since then, we have also published *Logit Modeling: Practical Applications* (DeMaris, No. 86), *Interpreting Probability Models: Logit, Probit, and Other Generalized Linear Models* (Liao, No. 101), and *Applied Logistic Regression Analysis* (Menard, No. 106), not to mention others which look at log linear models in contingency tables.

Given all the attention writers and researchers have given to logit modeling, one might ask if another treatment is necessary. The answer is "yes," if it is the right one, such as the volume at hand. For the budding researcher, logistic regression is tough going in comparison to OLS. Running logit is easy enough, for it is now in virtually all statistical packages. However, why run it? In addition, what do the results mean? These are questions that the conscientious methods teacher takes to heart because the subject, in its usual explication, appears complicated. What is needed is a primer, something for the newcomer who has recently mastered OLS. That is the sort of introduction Professor Pampel provides us here.

The first chapter dwells on the logic of logistic regression, when the dependent variable is dichotomous. In that circumstance, ordinary regression confronts multiple problems—nonlinearity, nonsense prediction, nonnormality, heteroskedasticity—which lead to inefficient estimation. Transforming the binary dependent variable into a logit allows this inefficiency to be overcome. Professor Pampel explains the components of the logit (a log of the odds of Y taking place), and how it works, along the way providing an especially useful appendix on the meaning of logarithms. (I have found that students coming to the material fresh always need a review of logarithms. Now they have it in convenient accompaniment).

The second chapter, on interpreting results, composes the meat of the monograph. It is with respect to interpretation that most textbook expositions have floundered. The central issue is, "What is the effect of X?" In OLS, this is answered in summary fashion, by the regression slope. Things are not so straightforward with logistic regression. Essentially, there are three possibilities. First, the slope estimate can be used directly to indicate the expected change in the logit, for a unit change in X. The difficulty with that is that it has little intuitive meaning. Second, the coefficient can be transformed to indicate the change in the odds (rather than the log odds) for a unit change in X. This is clearly a gain in meaning over the first strategy. Third, effects can be described in terms of probabilities. For example, if X changes +1 standard deviation from a baseline value, say its mean, then the probability of Y taking place increases by a calculable amount. The difficulty with this interpretation is that the effect of X can only be considered from a specific set of X values, rather than from a general unit change in X. These, and other difficulties, are evaluated in the volume.

The estimation procedure for ordinary regression is least squares. With a binary Y, however, least squares is no longer an efficient estimator, due to intrinsic nonlinearities. Therefore, the preferred procedure is maximum likelihood estimation (MLE), which our author explicates for the novice in Chapter 3, eventually presenting good coverage of model fit, still an area of some controversy. A further controversy, laid to rest in Chapter 4, is whether to use probit rather than logit. After spelling out the similarities and differences of the two methods, a convincing case is made for the use the latter over the former. Overall, for the research worker seeking an excellent initial accounting of the popular technique of logistic regression, the Pampel volume is the one to read.

—*Michael S. Lewis-Beck*
Series Editor

PREFACE

I call this book a primer because it makes explicit what treatments of logistic regression often take for granted. Some treatments explain concepts abstractly, assuming readers have a comfortable familiarity with odds and logarithms, maximum likelihood estimation, and non-linear functions. Other treatments skip the logical undergirding of logistic regression by proceeding directly to examples and the interpretation of actual coefficients. As a result, students sometimes fail to gain an understanding of the intuitive logic behind logistic regression. This book aims to introduce this logic with elementary language and simple examples.

Toward that end, Chapter 1 briefly presents a nontechnical explanation of the problems of using linear regression with dichotomous dependent variables, and then more thoroughly introduces the logit transformation. Chapter 2 presents central material on interpreting logistic regression coefficients. Chapter 3 takes up the meaning of maximum likelihood estimation, and the explanatory power of models in logistic regression. Chapter 4 reviews probit analysis, a similar way to analyze a binary dependent variable. Chapter 5, the conclusion, briefly considers how the fundamentals of logistic regression apply to nominal dependent variables with three or more categories. Because the basic logic of logistic regression applies to the extensions in the last chapters, none of the later topics gets the detailed discussion that logistic regression gets in Chapters 1 to 3. Finally, the Appendix reviews the meaning of logarithms, and may help some students understand the use of logarithms in logistic regression as well as in ordinary regression.

To Seth

LOGISTIC REGRESSION: A PRIMER

FRED C. PAMPEL
University of Colorado, Boulder

1. THE LOGIC OF LOGISTIC REGRESSION

Many social phenomena are discrete or qualitative rather than continuous or quantitative in nature—an event occurs or it does not occur, a person makes one choice but not the other, an individual or group passes from one state to another. A person can have a child, die, move (either within or across national borders), marry, divorce, enter or exit the labor force, receive welfare benefits, have their income fall below the poverty level, vote for one candidate, favor or oppose an issue, commit a crime, be arrested, quit school, enter college, join an organization, get sick, belong to a religion, or act in myriad ways that either involve a characteristic, event, or choice. Likewise, large social units—groups, organizations, and nations—can emerge, break up, go bankrupt, face rebellion, join larger groups, or pass from one type of discrete state into another.

Binary discrete phenomena usually take the form of a dichotomous indicator or dummy variable. Although it is possible to represent the two values with any numbers, employing variables with values of 1 and 0 has advantages. The mean of a dummy variable equals the proportion of cases with a value of 1, and can be interpreted as a probability.

Regression With a Dummy Dependent Variable

A binary qualitative dependent variable with values of 0 and 1 seems suitable on the surface for use with multiple regression. Regression coefficients have a useful interpretation with a dummy dependent variable—they show the increase or decrease in the predicted probability of having a characteristic or experiencing an event due to a

1

one-unit change in the independent variables. Equivalently, they show the change in the predicted proportion of respondents with a value of 1 due to a one-unit change in the independent variables. Given familiarity with proportions and probabilities, researchers should feel comfortable with such interpretations.

The dependent variable itself only takes values of 0 and 1, but the predicted values for regression take the form of mean proportions or probabilities conditional on the values of the independent variables. The higher the predicted value or conditional mean, the more likely that any individual with particular scores on the independent variables will have a characteristic or experience the event. Linear regression assumes that the conditional proportions or probabilities define a straight line for values of X.

To give a simple example, the 1994 General Social Survey (GSS) of the National Opinion Research Corporation asked respondents if they smoke. Assigning those who smoke a score of 1 and those who do not a score of 0 creates a dichotomous dependent variable. Taking smoking (S) as a function of years of completed education (E) and a dummy variable for gender (G) with females coded 1 produces the regression equation:

$$S = .661 - .029 * E + .004 * G.$$

The coefficient for education indicates that for a 1-year increase in education, the probability of smoking goes down by .029, the proportion smoking goes down by .029, or the percent smoking goes down by 2.9. Male respondents with no education have a predicted probability of smoking of .661 (the intercept). A male with 10 years of education has a predicted probability of smoking of .371 $(.661 - .029 * 10)$. One could also say that the model predicts 37% of such respondents smoke. The dummy variable coefficient shows females have a probability of smoking .004 higher than for males. With no education, women have a predicted probability of smoking of .665 $(.661 + .004)$.

Despite the uncomplicated interpretation of the coefficients for regression with a dummy dependent variable, the regression estimates face two sorts of problems. One type of problem is conceptual in nature, while the other type is statistical in nature. Together, the problems prove serious enough to require use of an alternative to ordinary regression with qualitative dependent variables.

Problems of Functional Form

The conceptual problem with linear regression with a dichotomous dependent variable stems from the fact that probabilities have maximum and minimum values of 1 and 0. By definition, probabilities and proportions cannot exceed 1 or fall below 0. Yet, the linear regression line can extend upward toward positive infinity as the values of the independent variables increase indefinitely, and extend downward toward negative infinity as the values of the independent variables decrease indefinitely. Depending on the slope of the line and the observed X values, a model can give predicted values of the dependent variable above 1 and below 0. Such values make no sense, and have little predictive use.

A few charts can illustrate the problem. The normal scatterplot of two continuous variables shows a cloud of points as in Figure 1.1(a). Here, a line through the middle of the cloud of points would minimize the sum of squared deviations. Further, at least theoretically, as X extends on to higher or lower levels, so does Y. The same straight line can predict large Y values associated with large X values as it can for medium or small values. The scatterplot of a relationship of a continuous independent variable to a dummy dependent variable in Figure 1.1(b), however, does not portray a cloud of points. It instead shows two parallel sets of points. Fitting a straight line seems less appropriate here. Any line (except one with a slope of zero) will eventually exceed 1 and fall below 0.

Some parts of the two parallel sets of points may contain more cases than others, and certain graphing techniques reveal the density of cases along the two lines. Jittering reduces overlap of the scatterplot points by adding random variation to each case. In Figure 1.2, the jittered distribution for a binary dependent variable—smokes or does not smoke—by years of education suggests a slight relationship. Cases with higher education appear less likely to smoke than cases with lower education. Still, Figure 1.2 differs from plots between continuous variables.

The risk of predicted probabilities below 0 or above 1 can, depending also on the range of values of the independent variable, increase with the skew of the dichotomous dependent variable. With a split of around 50:50, predicted values tend to fall toward the center of the probability distribution. In the previous example of smoking (where the split equals 28:72), the lowest predicted value of .081 occurs for

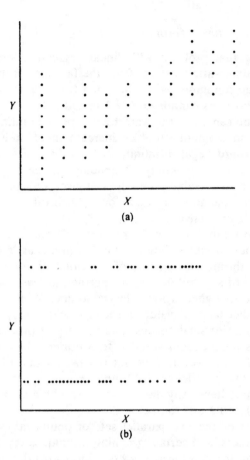

Figure 1.1. (a) Scatterplot, continuous variables, (b) scatterplot, dummy dependent variable.

males with the maximum education of 20; the highest predicted value of .665 occurs for females with the minimum education of 0. A more skewed dependent variable from the GSS asks respondents if they are a member of any group that aims to protect or preserve the environment. With the 10% saying yes coded 1 and others coded 0, a regression on education and gender gives

$$B = -.024 + .008 * E - .006 * G.$$

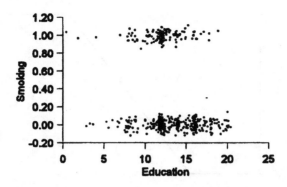

Figure 1.2. Jittered scatterplot for a binary dependent variable, smoking or nonsmoking by years of education.

The intercept shows the nonsensical probability that a male with no education will have a predicted probability of belonging below zero. Although a problem in general, reliance on the assumption of linearity in this particular model proves particularly inappropriate.[1]

One solution to the boundary problem would assume that any value equal to or above 1 should be truncated to the maximum value of 1. The regression line would be straight until this maximum value, but afterward changes in X would have no influence on the dependent variable. The same would hold for small values, which could be truncated at 0. Such a pattern would define sudden discontinuities in the relationship, whereby at certain points the effect of X on Y would change immediately to 0 (see Figure 1.3(a)).

However, another functional form of the relationship might make more theoretical sense than truncated linearity. With a floor and a ceiling, it seems likely that the effect of a unit change in the independent variable on the predicted probability would be smaller near the floor or ceiling than near the middle. Toward the middle of a relationship, the nonlinear curve may approximate linearity, but rather than continuing upward or downward indefinitely, the nonlinear curve bends slowly and smoothly so as to approach 0 and 1. As values get closer and closer to 0 or 1, the relationship requires a larger and larger change in the independent variable to have the same impact as a smaller change in the independent variable at the middle of the curve. To produce a change in the probability of experiencing an event from .95 to .96 requires a larger change in X than it does to produce

6

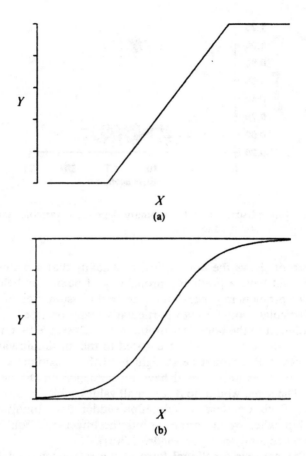

Figure 1.3. (a) Truncated linear relationship, (b) S-shaped curve.

a change in the probability from .45 to .46. The general principle is that the same additional input has less impact on the outcome near the ceiling or floor, and that increasingly larger inputs are needed to have the same impact on the outcome near the ceiling or floor.

Several examples illustrate the nonlinear relationship. If income increases the likelihood of owning a home, an increase of 10 thousand dollars of income from $40,000 to $50,000 would increase that likelihood more than an increase from $200,000 to $210,000. High-income persons would no doubt already have a high probability of home ownership, and a $10,000 increase would do little to increase their already high probability. The same would hold for an increase in income from $0 to $10,000: since neither income is likely to be sufficient to purchase a house, the increase in income has little impact on ownership. In the middle-range, however, the additional $10,000 may make the difference between being able to afford a house and not being able to afford a house.

Similarly, an increase of 1 year in age on the likelihood of first marriage may have much stronger effects during the late teens and early twenties than at younger or older ages. Few will marry under age 15 despite growing a year older, and few unmarried by 50 will likely marry by age 51. However, the change from age 21 to 22 may result in a substantial increase in the likelihood of marriage. The same kind of reasoning would apply in numerous other instances: the effect of the number of delinquent peers on the likelihood of committing a serious crime, the effect of the hours worked by women on the likelihood of having a child, the effect of the degree of party identification on the support for a political candidate, and the effect of drinking behavior on premature death are all likely stronger at the midrange of the independent variables than the extremes.

A more appropriate nonlinear relationship would look like that in Figure 1.3(b), where the curve levels off and approaches the ceiling of 1 and the floor of 0. Approximating the curve would require a succession of straight lines, each with different slopes. The lines nearer the ceiling and floor would have smaller slopes than those in the middle. However, a constantly changing curve more smoothly and adequately represents the relationship. Conceptually, the S-shaped curve makes better sense than the straight line.

Within a range of a sample, the linear regression line may approximate a curvilinear relationship by taking the average of the diverse slopes implied by the curve. However, the linear relationship still understates the actual relationships in the middle, and overstates the relationship at the extremes (unless the independent variable has values only in a region where the curve is nearly linear). Figure 1.4 compares the S-shaped curve with the straight line; the gap between the two illustrates the nature of the error, and the potential inaccuracy of linear regression.

The ceiling and floor create another conceptual problem besides nonlinearity in regression models of a dichotomous response. Regression typically assumes additivity—that the effect of one variable on the dependent variable stays the same regardless of the levels of

8

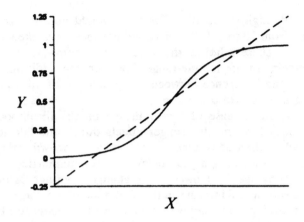

Figure 1.4. Linear versus curvilinear relationship.

the other independent variables. Models can include selected product terms to account for nonadditivity, but a dichotomous dependent variable likely violates the additivity assumption for all combinations of the independent variables. If the value of one independent variable reaches a sufficiently high level to push the probability of the dependent variable to near 1 (or to near 0), then the effects of other variables cannot have much influence. Thus, the ceiling and floor make the influence of all the independent variables inherently nonadditive and interactive.

To return to the smoking example, those persons with 20 years of education have such a low probability of smoking that only a small difference can exist between men and women; in other words, sex can have little effect on smoking at high levels of education. In contrast, larger sex differences likely exist when education is lower and the probability of smoking is higher. Although the effect of sex on smoking likely varies with the level of education, additive regression models incorrectly assume that the effect of sex on smoking is identical for all levels of education (and the effect of education is identical for both sexes).

Problems of Statistical Inference

Even if a straight line approximates the nonlinear relationship in some instances, some problems emerge that, despite leaving the estimates unbiased, reduce their efficiency. The problems involve the fact that regression with a dummy dependent variable violates the assumptions of normality and homoscedasticity. Both these problems stem from the existence of only two observed values for the dependent variable. Linear regression assumes that in the population a normal distribution of error values around the predicted Y is associated with each X value, and that the dispersion of the error values for each X value is the same. The assumptions imply normal and similarly dispersed error distributions.

Yet, with a dummy variable, only two Y values and only two residuals exist for any single X value. For any value X_i, the predicted probability equals $b_0 + b_1 X_i$. Therefore, the residuals take the value of

$$1 - (b_0 + b_1 X_i) \text{ when } Y_i \text{ equals } 1,$$

and

$$0 - (b_0 + b_1 X_i) \text{ when } Y_i \text{ equals } 0.$$

Even in the population, the distribution of errors for any X value cannot be normal when the distribution has only two values.

The error term also violates the assumption of homoscedasticity or equal variances because the regression error term varies with the value of X.[2] To illustrate this graphically, review Figure 1.1(b), which plots the relationship between X and a dichotomous dependent variable. Fitting a straight line that goes from the lower left to the upper right of the figure would define residuals as the vertical distance from the points to the line. Near the lower and upper extremes of X, where the line comes close to the floor of 0 and the ceiling of 1, the residuals are relatively small. Near the middle values of X, where the line falls halfway between the ceiling and floor, the residuals are relatively large. As a result, the variance of the errors is not constant.

While normality creates few problems with large samples, heteroscedasticity has more serious implications. The sample estimates of the population regression coefficients are unbiased, but they no longer have the smallest variance and the sample estimates of the standard errors are biased. Thus, even with large samples, the standard errors in the presence of heteroscedasticity will be incorrect, and tests of significance will be invalid. Technical means of weighing least squares estimates can deal with this problem, but more importantly do not solve the conceptual problems of nonlinearity and nonadditivity. Use of regression with a dummy dependent variable consequently remains inappropriate.

Transforming Probabilities into Logits

Linear regression faces a problem in dealing with a dependent variable with a ceiling and a floor: the same change in X has a different effect on Y depending on how close the curve corresponding to any X value comes to the maximum or minimum Y value. We need a transformation of the dependent variable to allow for the decreasing effects of X on Y as the predicted Y value approaches the floor or ceiling. We need, in other words, to eliminate the floor and ceiling inherent in probabilities.

Although many nonlinear functions can represent the S-shaped curve, the logistic or logit transformation, because of its desirable properties and relative simplicity, has become popular. To illustrate the logit transformation, assume that each case has a probability of having a characteristic or experiencing an event, defined as P_i. Since the dependent variable has values of only 0 and 1, this P_i must be estimated, but it helps to treat the outcome in terms of probabilities for now. Given this probability, the logit transformation involves two steps. First, take the ratio of P_i to $1 - P_i$, or the odds of experiencing the event. Second, take the natural logarithm of the odds. The logit thus equals

$$L_i = \ln[P_i/(1 - P_i)],$$

or, in short, the logged odds.

For example, if P_i equals .2 for the first case, its odds equals .25 or .2/.8, and its logit equals -1.386, the natural log of the odds. If P_i for the second case equals .7, its odds equal 2.33 or .7/.3, and its logit equals 0.847. If P_i equals .9 for the third case, its odds equals 9 or .9/.1, and its logit equals 2.197. Although the computational formula to transform probabilities into logits is straightforward, it requires some explanation to show its usefulness. It turns out to describe the relationship between independent variables and a distribution of probabilities defined by a dichotomous dependent variable.

Meaning of Odds

The logit begins by transforming probabilities into odds. Probabilities vary between 0 and 1, and express the likelihood of an event as a proportion of both occurrences and nonoccurrences. Odds express the likelihood of an occurrence relative to the likelihood of a nonoccurrence. Both probabilities and odds have a lower limit of zero, and both express the increasing likelihood of an event with increasing large positive numbers, but otherwise they differ.

Unlike a probability, odds have no upper bound or ceiling. As a probability gets closer to 1, the numerator of the odds becomes larger relative to the denominator, and the odds become an increasingly large number. The odds thus increase greatly when the probabilities change only slightly near their upper boundary of 1. For example, probabilities of .99, .999, .9999, .99999, and so on result in odds of 99, 999, 9999, 99999, and so on. Tiny changes in probabilities result in huge changes in the odds, and show that the odds increase toward infinity as the probabilities come closer and closer to 1.

To illustrate the relationship between probabilities and odds, examine the values

P_i	.01	.1	.2	.3	.4	.5	.6	.7	.8	.9	.99
$1 - P_i$	.99	.9	.8	.7	.6	.5	.4	.3	.2	.1	.01
Odds	.01	.111	.25	.429	.667	1	1.5	2.33	4	9	99.

Note that when the probability equals .5, the odds equal 1 or are even. As the probabilities increase toward one, the odds no longer have the ceiling of the probabilities. As the probabilities decrease toward zero, however, the odds still approach zero. At least at one end, then, the transformation allows values to extend linearly beyond the previous limit.

Manipulating the formula for odds gives further insight into their relationship to probabilities. Beginning with the definition of odds (O_i) as the ratio of the probability to one minus the probability, we can with simple algebra express the probability in terms of odds:

$$P_i/(1 - P_i) = O_i \text{ implies that } P_i = O_i/(1 + O_i).$$

The probability equals the odds divided by one plus the odds.[3]

Based on this formula, the probability can never equal or exceed one: no matter how large the odds become in the numerator, they will always be smaller by one than the denominator. Of course, as the odds become large, the gap between the odds and the odds plus 1 will become relatively small and the probability will approach (but not reach) one. Conversely, the probability can never fall below 0. As long as the odds equal or exceed 0, the probability must equal or exceed zero. The smaller the odds in the numerator become, the larger the relative size of the 1 in the denominator. The probability comes closer and closer to zero as the odds come closer and closer to 0.

Usually, the odds are expressed as a single number, taken implicitly as a ratio to 1. Thus, odds of 10 imply an event will occur 10 times for each time it does not occur. Since the single number can be a fraction, there is no need to keep both the numerator or denominator as a whole number. The odds of 7 to 3 can be expressed equally well as a single number of 2.33 (to 1). Thus, even odds equal 1 (1 occurrence to 1 nonoccurrence). Odds below 1 mean the event is less likely to occur than it is to not occur. If the probability equals .3, the odds are .3/.7 or .429. This means the event occurs .429 times per each time it does not occur. It could also be expressed as 42.9 occurrences per 100 nonoccurrences.

Expressed as a single number, any odds can be compared to another odds. Odds of 9 to 1 are three times higher than odds of 3. Odds of 3 are one-third the size of odds of 9. Odds of .429 are .429 the size of even odds of 1, or half the size of odds of .858. In each example, one odds is expressed as a multiple of the other.

It is often useful to compare two different odds as a ratio. The ratio of odds of 8 and 2 equals 4, which shows that the odds of the former group are four times (or 400%) larger than for the latter group. If the odds ratio is below 1, then the odds of the first group are lower than the second group. An odds ratio of .5 means the odds of the first group are only half or 50% the size of the second group. The closer the odds ratio to zero, the lower the odds of the first group to the second. An odds ratio of one means the odds of both groups are identical. Finally, if the odds ratio is above one, the odds of the first group are higher than the second group. The greater the odds ratio, the higher the odds of the first group to the second.

To prevent confusion, keep in mind the distinction between odds and odds ratios. Odds refer to a ratio of probabilities, while odds ratios refer to ratios of odds (or a ratio of probability ratios). According to the 1994 GSS, for example, 29.5% of men and 13.1% of women own a gun, Since the odds of gun ownership for men equal .418 (.295:

.705), it indicates that around 4 men own a gun for 10 who do not. The odds of gun ownership for women equal .151 or about 1.5 women own a gun for 10 who do not. The ratio of odds of men to women equal .418: .151 or 2.77, which means that the odds of gun ownership are nearly three times higher for men than women.

In summary, reliance on odds rather than probabilities provides for meaningful interpretation of the likelihood of events, but eliminates the upper boundary. Odds will prove useful later in interpreting co-efficients, but note now that creating odds represents the first step of the logit transformation.

Logged Odds

Taking the natural log of the odds eliminates the floor of 0 much as transforming probabilities into odds eliminates the ceiling of 1. Taking the natural log of:

odds above 0, but below 1 produces negative numbers;
odds equal to 1 produces 0; and
odds above 1 produces positive numbers.

(The logs of values equal to or below zero do not exist; see the Appendix for an introduction to logarithms and their properties.)

The first property of the logit, then, is that, unlike a probability, it has no upper or lower boundary. The odds eliminate the upper boundary of probabilities, and the logged odds eliminate the lower bound of probabilities as well. To see this, if $P_i = 1$, the logit is undefined because the odds of 1/0 do not exist. As the probability comes closer and closer to 1, however, the logit moves toward positive infinity. If $P_i = 0$, the logit is undefined because the log of the odds of 0/1 or 0 does not exist. As the probability comes closer and closer to 0, however, the logit proceeds toward negative infinity. Thus, the logits vary from negative infinity to positive infinity. The problem of a ceiling and floor in the probabilities (or a floor in odds) disappears.

The second property is that the logit transformation is symmetric around the midpoint probability of .5. The logit when $P_i = .5$ is 0 (.5: .5 = 1, and the log of 1 equals 0). Probabilities below .5 result in negative logits because the odds fall below 1 and above 0; P_i is smaller than $1 - P_i$, thereby resulting in a fraction, and the log of a fraction results in a negative number (see the Appendix). Probabilities above .5 result in positive logits because the odds exceed one (P_i is larger than $1 - P_i$). Further, probabilities the same distance above and below .5 (e.g., .6 and .4, .7 and .3, .8 and .2) have the same logits, but different signs (e.g., the logits for the probabilities listed above equal, in order, .405 and −.405, .847 and −.847, 1.386 and −1.386). The distance of the logit from 0 reflects the distance of the probability from .5 (again noting, however, that the logits do not have boundaries as do the probabilities).

The third property is that the same change in probabilities translates into different changes in the logits. The simple principle is that as P_i comes closer to 0 and 1, the same change in the probability translates into a greater change in the logged odds. You can see this by example,

P_i	.1	.2	.3	.4	.5	.6	.7	.8	.9
$1 - P_i$	.9	.8	.7	.6	.5	.4	.3	.2	.1
Odds	.111	.25	.429	.667	1	1.5	2.33	4	9
Logit	−2.20	−1.39	−.847	−.405	0	.405	.847	1.39	2.20.

A change in probabilities of .1 from .5 to .6 (or from .5 to .4) results in a change of .405 in the logit, whereas the same probability change of .1 from .8 to .9 (or from .2 to .1) results in a change of .810 in the logit. The change in the logit for the same change in the probability is twice as large at this extreme as in the middle. To repeat, the general principle is that small differences in probabilities result in increasingly larger differences in logits when the probabilities are near the bounds of 0 and 1.

Linearizing the Nonlinear

It helps to view the logit transformation as linearizing the inherent nonlinear relationship between X and the probability of Y. We would expect the same change in X to have a smaller impact on the probability of Y near the floor or ceiling than near the midpoint. Because the logit expands or stretches the probabilities of Y at extreme values relative to the values near the midpoint, the same change in X comes to have similar effects throughout the range of the logit transformation of the probability of Y. Without a floor or ceiling, in other words, the logit can relate linearly to changes in X. One can now compute a linear relationship between X and the logit transformation. The logit transformation straightens out the nonlinear relationship between X and the original probabilities.

Conversely, the linear relationship between X and the logit implies a nonlinear relationship between X and the original probabilities. A unit change in the logit results in smaller differences in probabilities at high and low levels than at levels in the middle. Just as we translate probabilities into logits, we can translate logits into probabilities (the formula to do this is discussed shortly),

Logit	−3	−2	−1	0	1	2	3
P_i	.047	.119	.269	.5	.731	.881	.953
Change	—	.072	.150	.231	.231	.150	.072.

A one-unit change in the logit translates into a greater change in probabilities near the midpoint than near the extremes. In other words, linearity in logits defines a theoretically meaningful nonlinear relationship with the probabilities.

Obtaining Probabilities from Logits

The linear relationships between the independent variables and the logit dependent variable imply nonlinear relationships with probabilities. The linear relationship of X to the predicted logit appears in

$$\ln(P_i/1 - P_i) = b_0 + b_1 X_i.$$

To express the probabilities rather than the logit as a function of X, first take each side of the equation as an exponent. Since the logarithm of a number as an exponent equals the number itself (e of the $\ln X$ equals X), exponentiation or taking the exponential eliminates the logarithm on the left side of the equation:

$$P_i/1 - P_i = e^{b_0 + b_1 X_i} = e^{b_0} * e^{b_1 X_i}.$$

Further, the equation can be presented in multiplicative form because the exponential of $X + Y$ equals the exponential of X times the exponential of Y. Thus, the odds change as a function of the coefficients treated as exponents.

Solving for P_i gives the formula[4]:

$$P_i = \left(e^{b_0 + b_1 X_i}\right) / \left(1 + e^{b_0 + b_1 X_i}\right).$$

Since the logit L_i equals $b_0 + b_1 X_i$, we can replace the longer formula by L_i in the equation, remembering that L_i is the logged odds predicted by the value of X_i and the coefficients b_0 and b_1. Then

$$P_i = e^{L_i} / \left(1 + e^{L_i}\right).$$

This formula takes the probability as a ratio of the exponential of the logit to 1 plus the exponential of the logit. Given that e^{L_i} produces odds, the formula corresponds to the equation $P_i = O_i/(1 + O_i)$ presented earlier.

Moving from logits to exponents of logits to probabilities shows

L	−4.61	−2.30	−1.61	−.223	0	1.61	2.30	4.61	6.91
e^L	.01	.1	.2	.8	1	5	10	100	1000
$1 + e^L$	1.01	1.1	1.2	1.8	2	6	11	101	1001
P	.010	.091	.167	.444	.5	.833	.909	.990	.999.

Note first that the exponentials of the negative logits fall between 0 and 1, and that the exponentials of the positive logits exceed one. Note also that the ratio of the exponential to the exponential plus 1 will always fall below one—the denominator will always exceed the numerator by 1. However, as the exponential gets larger, the difference between the numerator and the denominator declines (in other words, the extra one unit in the denominator becomes increasingly small relative to the other value in the numerator). Further, the ratio can never fall below zero since the exponentials of both negative and positive numbers end up positive and since the ratio of two positive numbers always ends up positive. Given the boundaries of the probabilities, the example shows that the larger L, the larger e^L, and the larger P.

This transformation also demonstrates nonlinearity. For a one-unit change in X, L changes by a constant amount, but P does not. The exponents in the formula for P_i makes the relationship nonlinear. Consider an example. If $L_i = 2 + .3X_i$, the logged odds change by .3 for a one-unit change in X regardless of the level of X. If X changes from 1 to 2, L changes from $2 + .3$ or 2.3 to $2 + .3 * 2$ or 2.6. If X changes from 11 to 12, L changes from 5.3 to 5.6. In both cases, the change in L is identical. This defines linearity.

Take the same values of X, and the L values they give, and note the changes they imply in the probabilities:

X	1	2	11	12
L	2.3	2.6	5.3	5.6
e^L	9.97	13.46	200.3	270.4
$1 + e^L$	10.97	14.46	201.3	271.4
P	.909	.931	.995	.996
Change		.022		.001.

Hence, the same change in L due to a unit change in X results in a greater change in the probabilities at lower levels of X and P than at higher levels. The same would show at the other end of the probability distribution.

This nonlinearity between the logit and the probability creates a fundamental problem of interpretation. We can summarize the effect of X on the logit simply in terms of a single linear coefficient, but we cannot do the same with the probabilities: the effect of X on the probability varies with the value of X and the level of probability. The complications in interpreting the effects on probabilities require a separate chapter on the meaning of logistic regression coefficients. However, dealing with problems of interpretation proves easier having fully discussed the logic of the logit transformation.

An Alternative Formula

For purposes of calculation, the formula for probabilities as a function of the independent variables and coefficients takes a somewhat simpler, but less intuitive form:

$$P_i = e^{b_0+b_1X_i} / \left(1 + e^{b_0+b_1X_i}\right),$$
$$P_i = 1 / \left(1 + e^{-(b_0+b_1X_i)}\right),$$
$$P_i = 1 / \left(1 + e^{-L_i}\right).$$

In this formula, you need to take the exponential after taking the negative of the logit. The probability then equals 1 divided by 1 plus the exponential of the negative of the logit. This gives exactly the same result as the other formula.[5]

Either formula works to translate logits into probabilities. If the logit equals -2.302, then we must solve for $P = e^{-2.302}/1 + e^{-2.302}$ or $1/1 + e^{-(-2.302)}$. The exponential of -2.302 equals approximately .1, and the exponential of the negative of −2.302 or 2.302 equals 9.994. Thus, the probability equals .1/1.1 or .091, or calculated alternatively equals 1/1+9.994 or .091. The same calculations can be done for any other logit value to get probabilities.

Summary

This chapter reviews how the logit transforms a dependent variable having inherent nonlinear relationships with a set of independent variables into a dependent variable having linear relationships with a set of independent variables.[6] Logistic regression models (sometimes also called logit models) thus estimate the linear determinants of the logged odds or logit rather than the nonlinear determinants of probabilities. Obtaining these estimates involves complexities left until later chapters. In the meantime, however, it helps to view logistic regression in simple terms as regression on a dependent variable that transforms nonlinear relationships into linear relationships.

In linearizing the nonlinear relationships, logistic regression also shifts the interpretation of coefficients from changes in probabilities to less intuitive changes in logged odds. The loss of interpretability with the logistic coefficients, however, is balanced by the gain in parsimony: the linear relationship with the logged odds can be summarized with a single coefficient, but the nonlinear relationship with the probabilities cannot be so simply summarized. Efforts to interpret logistic regression coefficients in a meaningful, yet relatively simple way define the topic of the next chapter.

2. INTERPRETING LOGISTIC REGRESSION COEFFICIENTS

Although it simplifies the estimation issues to come, treating logistic regression as a form of regression on a dependent variable transformed into logged odds helps describe the underlying logic of the procedure. However, as is true for nonlinear transformations more generally, the effects of the independent variables in logistic regression have multiple interpretations. Effects exist for probabilities, odds, and logged odds, and the interpretations of each effect have both advantages and disadvantages.

To preview, the effects of the independent variables on the logged odds are linear and additive—each X variable has the same effect on the logged odds regardless of its level or the level of other X variables—but the units of the dependent variable, logged odds, have little intuitive meaning. The effects of the independent variables on the probabilities have intuitive meaning, but are nonlinear and nonadditive—each X variable has a different effect on the probability depending on its level and the level of the other independent variables. Despite the interpretable units, the effects on probabilities cannot be simply summarized in the form of a single coefficient.

The interpretation of the effects of the independent variables on the odds offers a compromise between the previous alternatives. The odds have more intuitive appeal than the logged odds, and can express effects in single coefficients. The effects on odds are multiplicative rather than additive, but still have a straightforward interpretation. Other ways to interpret the effects of the independent variables exist. The ratios of the coefficients to their standard errors obviously have importance in interpreting sample results. Also, various attempts to standardize the coefficients for the independent variables and compare their relative size may prove helpful.

This chapter examines each of these ways to interpret effects in logistic regression. Further, it examines the variations in each interpretation for continuous and dummy independent variables.

Logged Odds

The first interpretation directly uses the coefficients obtained from the estimates of the logistic regression. The logistic regression coefficients simply show the change in the predicted logged odds of experiencing an event or having a characteristic for a one-unit change in the independent variables. The coefficients have exactly the same interpretation as the coefficients in regression except that the units of the dependent variable represent the logged odds. For example, Browne (1997, p. 246) uses logistic regression to predict participation in the labor force of 922 female heads of household between ages 18 and 54 in 1989. The logistic regression coefficient of .13 for years employed shows that each additional year of employment increases the logged odds of current participation in the labor force by .13.

For dummy variables, a change in one unit implicitly compares the indicator group to the reference or omitted group. Browne uses dummy variables for high school dropouts and high school graduates to compare their labor force participation to those women with some college education (the reference group). The coefficients of −1.29 and −.68 for these two dummy variables indicate that the logged odds of being in the labor force are 1.29 lower for high school dropouts than for those with some college, and are .68 lower for high school graduates than for those with some college. Excepting the metric of the dependent variable, this interpretation represents nothing different from that used for dummy variables in ordinary regression.

These coefficients represent the relationship, as in ordinary regression, with a single coefficient. Regardless of the value of X—small, medium, or large—or the values of the other independent variables, a one-unit change has the same effect on the dependent variable. According to the model, the difference in the logged odds of participation between a woman with 1 year of experience and a woman with 2 years of experience equals the difference in the logged odds of participation between a woman with 21 years of experience and a woman with 22 years of experience. Similarly, the effect of years employed in the model does not differ between high school dropouts, high school graduates, and those with some college. All one needs to do is copy the coefficient from the printout. Indeed, logistic regression aims to simplify the nonlinear and nonadditive relationships inherent in treating probabilities as dependent variables.

Note also that logistic regression, as in linear regression, can include product terms to represent interactive relationships and polynomial terms to represent curvilinear relationships. The product and squared terms in logistic regression have much the same interpretation as in linear regression, except that the units of the dependent variable take the form of logged odds. Logistic regression already contains nonadditivity and nonlinearity in the relationships between the independent variables and probabilities, but can further model nonadditivity and nonlinearity in the relationship between the independent variables and the logged odds (DeMaris, 1992).

Despite the simplicity of their interpretation, the logistic regression coefficients, as mentioned, lack a meaningful metric. Statements about the effects of variables on changes in logged odds reveal little about the relationships and do little to help explain the substantive results. Researchers need means to interpret the substantive meaning or importance of the coefficients other than merely reporting the expected changes in logged odds.

Odds

The second interpretation comes from transforming the logistic regression coefficients so that the independent variables affect the odds rather than the logged odds of the dependent variable. To find the effects on the odds, simply take the exponent or antilogarithm of the logistic regression coefficients. As in the two variable model that follows, exponentiating both sides of the logistic regression equation eliminates the log of the odds and shows the influences of the variables on the odds,

$$\ln(P/1 - P) = b_0 + b_1 X_1 + b_2 X_2,$$
$$e^{\ln(P/1-P)} = e^{b_0 + b_1 X_1 + b_2 X_2},$$
$$P/1 - P = e^{b_0} * e^{b_1 X_1} * e^{b_2 X_2}.$$

As noted in the last chapter, the antilog of the log of a value equals the value itself, and the left side of the equation equals the odds. In addition, since the exponent of $(X + Y)$ equals the exponent of X times the exponent of Y, the right-hand side of the equation becomes multiplicative rather than additive.

The odds are a function of the exponentiated constant (e^{b_0}) multiplied by the exponentiated product of the coefficient and X_1($e^{b_1 X_1}$) and the exponentiated product of the coefficient and X_2($e^{b_2 X_2}$). In simple terms, the effect of each variable on the odds (rather than the logged odds) comes from taking the antilog of the coefficients. If not already presented in the computer output, the exponentiated coefficients can be obtained from most any calculator by typing the coefficient and then the e^x function. The exponentiated coefficients of .13, −1.29, and −.68 from Browne's study of women's labor force participation equal 1.14, .28, and .51.

The fact that the equation determining the odds is multiplicative rather than additive affects the interpretation of the exponentiated coefficients. In an additive equation, a variable has no effect when its coefficient equals 0. The predicted value of the dependent variable sums the values of the variables times the coefficients; when adding 0, the predicted value does not change. In a multiplicative equation, the predicted value of the dependent variable does not change when multiplied by a coefficient of 1. Therefore, 0 in the additive equation corresponds to 1 in the multiplicative equation. Further, the exponential of a positive number exceeds 1 and the exponential of a negative number falls below 1 (but above zero, as the exponential of any number is always greater than zero).

For the exponentiated coefficients, then, a coefficient of 1 leaves the odds unchanged, a coefficient greater than 1 increases the odds, and a coefficient smaller than 1 decreases the odds. Moreover, the more distant the coefficient from 1 in either direction, the greater the effect in changing the odds. For example, the exponentiated coefficient for years of employment, 1.14, indicates that a 1-year increase in employment multiplies the odds of labor force participation by 1.14 or increases the odds by a factor of 1.14. If the odds of participation for someone employed 12 years equals 4.88, the odds of participation for someone employed 13 years equals 4.88 * 1.14 or 5.56. The odds of participation for someone employed 14 years in turn equals 5.56 * 1.14 or 6.34.[7]

In terms of odds ratios, dividing the odds of someone with 13 years of experience by the odds of someone with 12 years of experience gives the exponentiated logistic regression coefficient: 5.56/4.48 = 1.14. Thus, the coefficient shows the ratio of odds for a one-unit increase in the independent variable.

For dummy variables, a similar interpretation follows. The exponentiated coefficient for the high school dropout dummy variable, .28, indicates that a one-unit increase in the variable multiplies the odds of labor force participation by .28. Of course, a one-unit increase compares high school dropouts to the reference group of those with some college. In either case, multiplying by .28 substantially lowers the odds. If the odds of participation for those with some college equal 15.6, the odds of participation for high school dropouts equal 15.6 * .28 or 4.37. For high school graduates, the exponentiated coefficient of .51 indicates that the odds of participation are .51 times smaller than for those with some college. Their odds would equal 15.6 * .51 or 7.96. In terms of odds ratios, the exponentiated coefficient for the dummy variable equals the ratio of odds for the dummy variable group to the odds for the reference group.

Since the distance of an exponentiated coefficient from 1 indicates the size of the effect, a simple calculation can further aid in interpretation. The difference of a coefficient from 1 exhibits the increase or decrease in the odds for a unit change in the independent variable. In terms of a formula, the exponentiated coefficient minus 1 and times 100 gives the percentage increase or decrease due to a one-unit change in the independent variable:

$$\%\Delta = (e^b - 1) * 100.$$

For years of employment, the exponentiated coefficient says that the odds of participating in the labor force increase by 14% for an increase of 1 year of employment experience. This appears more meaningful than to say the logged odds increase by .13.[8] The size of the effect on the odds also depends on the units of measurement of the independent variables—the change in odds for variables measured in different units do not warrant direct comparison. Still, the interpretation of percentage change in the odds has intuitive appeal.

Turning to the dummy variables, the percentage change of the exponentiated logistic regression coefficient for high school dropouts equals $(.28 - 1) * 100$ or -72. This means that the odds of participating are 72% lower for high school dropouts than for those with some college. The exponentiated coefficient for high school graduates of .51 indicates that their odds of participating are 49% lower than for those with some college.

In interpreting the exponentiated coefficients, remember that they refer to multiplicative changes in the odds rather than probabilities. It is easy to say that an additional year of work experience makes participation 1.14 times more probable or otherwise imply probabilities rather than odds (DeMaris, 1995, p. 1960). More precisely, the odds of participation are 1.14 times as large or 14% larger for an additional year of work.

Probabilities

The third strategy of interpreting the logistic regression coefficients involves translating the effects on logged odds or odds into the effects on probabilities. Since the relationships between the independent variables and probabilities are nonlinear and nonadditive, they cannot be fully represented by a single coefficient. The effect on the probabilities has to be identified at a particular value or set of values. The choice of values to use in evaluating the effect of variables on the probabilities depends on the concerns of the researcher and

24

the nature of the data, but an initial strategy has the advantage of simplicity: examine the effect on the probability for a typical case.

Continuous Independent Variables

One quick way to gauge the influence of a continuous variable on probabilities involves calculating the linear slope of the tangent of the nonlinear curve at any single point. The slope of the tangent line is defined by the partial derivative of the nonlinear equation relating the independent variables to the probabilities, but more intuitively represents a straight line that meets the logistic curve at a single point without crossing to the other side of the curve. Figure 2.1 depicts the tangent line where the logistic curve intersects $Y = P = .76$. The tangent line identifies the slope only at that particular point, but allows for easy interpretation. Its slope shows the linear change in the probability for a one-unit change in the independent variable defined at a single point on the logistic curve.

The change in probability or the linear slope of the tangent line comes from a simple equation for the partial derivative. The partial derivative reveals the change in the probability for an infinitely small change in X, but also defines the slope of the tangent line or the

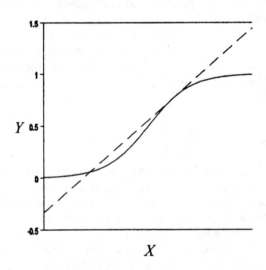

Figure 2.1. Tangent line of logistic curve at $Y = P = .76$.

change in the tangent line due to a one-unit change in X at that value (as discussed shortly, it does not equal the actual change in the logistic regression curve due to a one-unit change in X). The partial derivative, also referred to as the marginal or instantaneous effect, equals

$$\partial P / \partial X_k = b_k * P * (1 - P).$$

Simply multiply the logistic regression coefficient by the selected probability P and 1 minus the probability.

The formula for the partial derivative nicely reveals the nonlinear effects of an independent variable on probabilities. The effect of b (in terms of logged odds) translates into a different effect on the probabilities depending on the level of P. The effect will be at its maximum when P equals .5 since $.5*.5 = .25, .6*.4 = .24, .7*.3 = .21$ and so on. The closer P comes to the ceiling or floor, the smaller the value $P * (1 - P)$, and the smaller the effect a unit change in X has on the probability.

Multiplying the coefficient times $.5 * .5$ shows the maximum effect on the probabilities, but may overstate the influence for a sample in which the split on the dependent variable is not so even. Substituting the mean of the dependent variable, P, in the formula gives a more typical effect. In Browne's example, the logistic regression coefficient for years employed equals .13; the mean of the dependent variable, the expected probability of participating, equals .83; and the probability of not participating equals .17. Multiplying all three gives a value of .018. An increase of 1 year of employment increases the probability of participation by .018 or almost 2% at the mean. The effect reaches its maximum of .032 when $P = .5$.

As an alternative to the mean, we might compute the predicted probability for a typical case on the independent variables, and use that probability to calculate the partial derivative. Substituting the means of the continuous variables and the value of the modal category for dummy variables into the logistic regression equation yields the predicted logged odds for that case. Transforming the predicted logged odds into a predicted probability allows calculation of the effects on probabilities for that case.

In much the same way, a researcher might compute a predicted probability for a range of values on the independent variables and present the marginal effects for the extremes as well as the middle of the sample (Long, 1997, p. 64). Allowing all the other variables to take their mean values, calculate the predicted probabilities when one variable takes values −2, −1, 0, 1, and 2 standard deviations from the mean. Then use these probabilities to calculate marginal effects. Alternatively, calculate probabilities and the associated marginal effects when the independent variable takes its maximum, mean, and minimum values. Long (1997) discusses a number of others ways—including the use of both tables and graphs—to present a more complete summary of the range of influences of a variable on probabilities.

The formula for the partial derivative demonstrates the nonadditive as well as the nonlinear nature of the relationships with probabilities: the effect of one independent variable on the probabilities varies with P, and P varies with the values of other independent variables. When X_2 is at its mean, it might predict P near .5 and X_1 would have a relatively large marginal effect. When X_2 is near its maximum, it might predict a P near 1 and X_1 would have a relatively small marginal effect. The effect of X_1 on the probabilities, in other words, varies with the values of other independent variables and predicted P values. This means that the independent variables interact in determining probabilities (remember that the effects of the variables on the logged odds are linear and additive).

The inherent nonlinear and nonadditive influence of the determinants on probabilities limits the value of any single summary coefficient. Given the difficulties of describing a nonlinear and nonadditive relationship with a single coefficient, analysts disagree over whether it is valuable to even calculate a single partial derivative (DeMaris, 1990, 1993; Roncek, 1993). Critics of the procedure view the resulting coefficient as misleading, and little better than using linear regression. Even so, the tendency of researchers to think in terms of proportions or probabilities may warrant use of the slope of the tangent at the mean of the dependent variable or other points on the logistic curve as a supplement to other interpretations.

Dummy Independent Variables

The partial derivative works best with continuous variables for which small changes in the independent variables that define the tangent have meaning. For dummy variables, the relevant change occurs from 0 to 1, and the tangent line for small changes in X makes less sense. Instead, it is possible to compute predicted probabilities for each group, and then subtract the two probabilities to measure the group differences in probabilities. The partial derivative of the coefficient for a dummy variable may approximate the group difference in probabilities, but calculating the predicted probabilities gives the exact difference. Remember, however, that the calculated group difference in probabilities, like the partial derivative, varies with the point on the logistic curve, the X values, and the P values.

To make the calculation, select a starting probability from which to evaluate the effect of the dummy variable. With this value serving as the probability for the omitted group, calculate the predicted probability for the dummy variable group. Subtracting these two probabilities shows the difference in the probability between the two groups evaluated at the selected starting point (Peterson, 1985). The mean of the dependent variable may serve as the probability of the omitted group, but other values of special interest may work equally well as the starting point. Choosing other P values for the omitted group, although appropriate and useful, will produce different results.

More precisely, follow these steps. (a) Find the logged odds of P or the predicted logit for the omitted group. (b) To get the predicted logit for the dummy variable group, add the logistic regression coefficient to the predicted logit for the omitted group. (c) Compute the probability from the predicted logit for the dummy variable group using the formula listed below and in Chapter 1. (d) Subtract P from the probability for the dummy variable group to obtain the between-group difference in probabilities (or the effect of the dummy variable on probabilities).

In formula, the steps take the form,

$$L_o = \ln(P_o/(1 - P_o)) \text{ logit for the omitted group,}$$
$$L_d = L_o + b_d \text{ logit for the dummy variable group,}$$
$$P_d = 1/1 + e^{-L_d} \text{ probability for the dummy variable group,}$$
$$P_d - P_o \text{ difference in probabilities.}$$

In Browne's example, using the mean of the dependent variable or .83 as P_o and the b for high school dropouts of -1.29 (with women with some college serving as the omitted group), follow the previous steps,

$$L_o = \ln(P_o/(1 - P_o)) = \ln(.83/.17) = 1.586 \text{ logit for women}$$
with some college,

$L_d = L_o + b = 1.586 - 1.29 = .296$ logit for high school dropouts,

$P_d = 1/1 + e^{-L_d} = 1/1 + .7438 = .573$ probability for high school dropouts,

$P_d - P_o = .573 - .83 = -.257$ difference in probabilities.

Evaluated at the mean of the dependent variable, high school dropouts have a probability of participating that is .257 lower than those with some college education. As always, the formula translating logits into probabilities is nonlinear, and the difference in probabilities for the two groups will vary depending on the value of P and the other independent variables.

Predicted Probabilities for Continuous Independent Variables

Even for continuous independent variables, the partial derivative lends itself to potential misinterpretation: it shows the change in the *tangent line* for a one-unit change in the independent variable rather than the change in the *logistic curve* for a one-unit change in the independent variable. Note that in Figure 2.1, the tangent continues upward from P, while the logistic regression curve bends. Consequently, the changes in probabilities for a one-unit change in X differ for the tangent line and the logistic curve. Because the tangent represents a straight line, calculating its slope is easier than calculating the change in probabilities for the logistic curve, but it does not reflect the observed change in the probability for a unit change in X.

As an alternative to the partial derivative, predicted probabilities can be used for continuous variables much as for dummy variables. Changes in predicted probabilities indicate the actual effect of a discrete change in X—such as one unit—rather than the effect on the tangent line implied by an instantaneous or infinitely small change in X. For that reason, some prefer the use of predicted probabilities for a discrete change over the partial derivative (Kaufman, 1996; Long, 1997). However, use of predicted probabilities for discrete changes in X still depends on the point of the curve chosen to calculate the predicted probabilities. Given the nonlinear relationships between independent variables and probabilities, the effect of X on predicted probabilities will vary with the starting value of X.

The calculations for predicted probabilities follow the formulas used for dummy variables, only they substitute X for the omitted group and $X + 1$ for the dummy variable group. Using the mean of the dependent variable or some other value as a starting point for X, the procedure then calculates the predicted probability for $X + 1$. Subtracting the probabilities shows the effect of a one-unit change in X on the predicted probabilities. More precisely, first find the logged odds of P (i.e., the logit before the change in the independent variable). Then add the logistic regression coefficient for the variable to the starting logit and compute the probability for this new logit. Finally, subtracting the starting probability (at X) from the second probability (at $X + 1$) shows the effect of a one-unit change in X on the predicted probability at P.

In Browne's example, P equals .83 and the coefficient for years employment equals .13. The logit at P equals the log of .83/.17, or 1.586. Adding the coefficient to this logit gives 1.716 (1.586 + .13). Using the formula for probabilities as a function of logits ($P = 1/1 + e^{-L}$), the probability for $X + 1$ equals .848. The difference between .848 and .83 equals .018. A one-unit increase in years of employment increases the probability of labor force participation by .018 at the mean of the dependent variable. In this case, the discrete and instantaneous change in X show the same change in probabilities to three decimal places, but in other cases they will produce larger differences (e.g., Kaufman, 1996).

To illustrate the influence of the starting value, consider another calculation. Beginning with a P of .5 gives a logit of 0, adding the logistic regression coefficient gives .13, and computing the probability of the .13 logit gives .532. The effect of .532 −.5 thus equals .032— nearly twice the size of the effect at $P = .83$. As discussed earlier, besides using the mean of the dependent variable as a starting value, one can use the predicted probability based on the means of all continuous variables and the modal categories of the dummy variables. As also discussed earlier, one could even deal with the nonlinearity of effects on probabilities by calculating a *set* of effects on probabilities defined by various values of the independent variables.[9]

The variety of ways to interpret the effects on probabilities indicates the difficulty in summarizing nonlinear relationships. Some recommend avoiding these types of interpretations altogether, and focusing on the multiplicative changes in the odds rather than on changes in probabilities. When focusing on probabilities, however, the quickest and easiest calculations involve the partial derivatives for continuous variables and differences in predicted probabilities for dummy variables computed at the mean probability for the sample. For more detail, using marginal effects or predicted probability effects at a variety of points on the curve may prove useful.

Tests of Significance

Because tests of significance in logistic regression differ little from those in ordinary regression, they do not require the detailed discussion of the coefficients. Like in regression, the size of the coefficient relative to its standard error provides the basis for tests of significance in logistic regression. The logistic regression program in STATA presents the coefficient divided by its standard error, which can be evaluated with the z distribution. The significance of the coefficient—the likelihood that the coefficient in the sample could have occurred by chance alone when the population parameter equals 0—is then interpreted as usual. However, since we know little about the small sample properties of logistic regression coefficients, tests of significance for samples less than 100 prove risky (Long, 1997, p. 54).

The logistic regression programs in SPSS® and SAS® calculate the Wald statistic for a (two-tailed) test of a single coefficient, which equals the square of the ratio of the coefficient divided by its standard error and has a chi-square distribution. Besides the caveat concerning sample size, another potential problem affects the Wald statistic (Long, 1997, pp. 97–98). With a large absolute value for the logistic regression coefficient, the estimated standard error may lack precision because of rounding error, and provide an incorrect test of the null hypothesis. In such cases, comparing the log likelihood ratio (discussed in the next chapter) for models with and without the variable can test for its significance.

Coefficients should exceed standard levels of significance before applying the interpretations discussed in the previous sections. Because statistical significance depends so strongly on sample size, however, p values provide little information on the strength, importance, or intuitive meaning of the relationship. Large samples, in particular, can produce significant p values for otherwise small and unimportant effects. Despite the common reliance of studies on statistical significance (and the sign of the coefficient) as the dominant means of interpreting logistic regression coefficients, p values should serve only as an initial hurdle to overcome before interpreting the coefficient in other ways.

Raftery (1995) has recently developed a way to deal with the unsatisfactory results of traditional hypothesis testing in large samples. He proposes a Bayesian information criterion (BIC) for a variety of statistical tests. Applied to individual logistic regression coefficients, the BIC differs from p values. Based on some complex derivations and approximations, Raftery (1995, p. 139) suggests that, to reject the null hypothesis, the squared t or, in this case, the squared z and chi-square value for a coefficient should exceed the logarithm of the sample size. In terms of formula, the BIC value,

$$BIC = z^2 - \ln n,$$

should exceed zero to reach significance. Specifically, the BIC value refers to the difference in model information with and without the variable and coefficient in question. If the BIC value for a variable equals or falls below 0, the data provide little support for including the variable in the model. In equivalent terms, the absolute value of z should exceed $\sqrt{\ln n}$.

For coefficients with BIC differences above zero, Raftery specifies a rule of thumb to evaluate the "grades of the evidence" for the inclusion of a variable. He defines a BIC difference of 0–2 as weak, 2–6 as positive, 6–10 as strong, and greater than 10 as very strong. By formalizing a way to evaluate null hypotheses for samples of varied sizes, the BIC test of significance for a coefficient provides more information than traditional significance tests. It proves especially helpful to logistic regression, where coefficients measured in terms of logged odds do not offer an easy measure of strength.

In Browne's analysis, years employed has a standard error of .02 for the logistic regression coefficient of .13. A z value of 6.5 and a chi-square value 42.25 easily meet the .01 probability level. The z and chi-square values for the high school dropout dummy variable equal 4.45 and 19.8, again easily meeting standard significance levels. In addition, the log of the sample size of 922 equals 6.83. The BIC values (i.e., $42.25 - 6.83 = 35.42$, and $19.8 - 6.83 = 12.97$) for the two variables fall into the very strong range.

Standardized Coefficients

Regression ordinarily multiplies unstandardized coefficients by the ratio of the standard deviation of X to the standard deviation of Y to obtain standardized coefficients. The product gives coefficients identical to those that would be obtained if, before being entered into the regression program, the variables were first transformed into standard scores (with means of 0 and standard deviations of 1). Unlike multiple regression programs, logistic regression programs do not routinely compute standardized coefficients. The problem with standardized coefficients in logistic regression stems partly from ambiguity in the meaning of standard scores or standard units for dummy variables. Standardized dummy variables merely translate values of 0 and 1 into two other values. If the mean of the dependent variable equals the probability P, the variance equals $P * (1 - P)$. Then,

$$Y \text{ values of 1 have } z \text{ values equal to } (1 - P)/\sqrt{P * (1 - P)},$$

and

$$Y \text{ values of 0 have } z \text{ values equal to } (0 - P)/\sqrt{P * (1 - P)}.$$

With only two values, a standardized dummy variable does not represent a matter of degree and reference to a standard deviation change lacks concrete reference. Because a standard deviation change in a binary variable therefore typically does not have the same meaning as a standard deviation change in a continuous variable, some avoid the use of standardized coefficients for dummy variables.

More importantly for logistic regression with a dummy dependent variable, the model predicts the logged odds, a transformation which represents a dependent variable without bounds and with an arbitrarily defined variance. No simple and obvious standard deviation exists for logits, and no simple standardization exists for the dependent variable in logistic regression.

Standardizing only the independent variables before using them in the logistic regression presents no problems. The resulting coefficients show the change in the logged odds of experiencing an event or having a characteristic due to a one standard deviation change in each of the independent variables. With a comparable metric for the independent variables, these semistandardized coefficients reflect the relative importance of variables within an equation. Alternatively, multiplying by hand the logistic regression coefficient for independent variables in their original metric by the standard deviation of the variables gives the same result.[10]

Such comparisons identify the effects of different independent variables for the same dependent variable. However, without standardizing the dependent variable as well, the coefficients do not have the same interpretation as fully standardized coefficients. Indeed, without standardizing both the dependent and independent variables, comparison of the effects of independent variables on different dependent variables can be misleading. A fully standardized coefficient, B_{yx}^*, would adjust for the standard deviations of both X and Y as in the formula

$$B_{yx}^* = b_{yx}(s_x/s_y).$$

where b_{yx} equals the logistic regression coefficient, s_x equals the standard deviation of X and s_y equals the standard deviation of Y. However, the problem of how to obtain the standard deviation of Y remains.

Logistic regression in SPSS calculates an analogous partial correlation coefficient that varies from -1 to $+1$. The partial correlation coefficients are computed from the Wald statistic and the baseline log likelihood ratio (discussed in the next chapter); when the Wald statistic falls below 2, SPSS sets the partial correlation to zero. Yet, partial correlation coefficients differ from standardized regression coefficients, and do not correspond exactly to measures used in regression.

SAS prints standardized coefficients for logistic regression. The program uses the standard deviation of the logit distribution (1.8138 or the square root of $\pi^2/3$) as the standard deviation of the dependent variable. This standard deviation does not consider the distribution of the actual dependent variable, but assumes it is the same for all equations. Again, such a coefficient does not duplicate the usual standardized coefficients in regression.

To obtain a more meaningful measure of the standard deviation of an actual dependent variable, Long (1997) recommends using the predicted logits. Logistic regression transforms the probabilities based on a dichotomous dependent variable into logged odds to represent an underlying continuous variable. The predicted logged odds from logistic regression have an observed variance. In addition, the error term in the logistic regression equation has a variance, arbitrarily defined in the logistic distribution as $\pi^2/3$. Together, the variance of the predicted logits plus the variance of the error term offers an estimate of the variance of the unobserved continuous dependent variable. Taking the square root of the variance provides a measure of the standard deviation of the continuous latent variable. Using this standard deviation in the formula for the standardized coefficient will show that the logged odds change by B_{yx}^* standard deviation units for a one standard deviation unit change in X.

To estimate s_y, save the predicted logit values for each case from the logistic regression. Since the predicted values have a distribution, a command for descriptive statistics will report the variance. If the logistic regression program, as in SPSS, saves the predicted probabilities, compute the logged odds from the predicted probabilities and obtain the variance of the logged odds. Then add to this variance the variance of the error term, defined in logistic regression as 3.2899, and take the square root of the sum to obtain a measure of the standard deviation of the dependent variable. Note that this estimate of the standard deviation depends on the predicted values and therefore on the particular specification of the model. Unlike the standard deviation for a dependent variable in regression, the standard deviation will change with new independent variables.

Menard (1995, p. 46) suggests another way to indirectly estimate the standard deviation of the logged odds. In regression, the variance explained equals the regression sum of squares divided by the total sum of squares. Once dividing the two sum of squares by the sample size of n (or $n - 1$), the variance explained equals the variance of the predicted values of the dependent variable divided by the variance of the dependent variable:

$$R^2 = SS_{\text{reg}}/SS_{\text{tot}} = (SS_{\text{sreg}}/n)(SS_{\text{tot}}/n) = s_{\text{reg}}^2/s_y^2.$$

Through simple algebra, the variance of Y equals the variance of the predicted regression values over the variance explained, and the standard deviation of Y equals the square root of the ratio.

In summary form, the steps to computing this standardized coefficient follow:

1. Save the predicted probabilities from logistic regression or save the predicted logits and transform them into probabilities;
2. Correlate the predicted probabilities with the dummy dependent variable to obtain R and R^2;
3. Transform the predicted probabilities into predicted logits or use the predicted logits directly;
4. Find the variance of the predicted logits;
5. Compute the standard deviation of Y as the square root of the variance of the predicted logits divided by R^2; and
6. With the estimated standard deviation of Y, the standard deviation of X, and the logistic regression coefficient, compute the standardized coefficient. The resulting coefficient shows the standard deviation change in the logit for a one standard deviation change in an independent variable.

An Example

To review the variety of interpretations of logistic regression coefficients, I consider a simple model of smoking using the 1994 General Social Survey. The logistic regression includes four independent variables: education in years of completed formal schooling; age in years since birth; a dummy variable for sex with females coded 1; and a dummy variable for marital status with married persons coded 1. The sample includes 510 respondents with valid data on smoking and the four independent variables. Table 2.1 presents partial output from the SPSS logistic regression.

TABLE 2.1
Partial SPSS Logistic Regression Results: Variable Coefficients

Variable	B	S.E.	Wald	df	Sig	R	Exp(B)
Education	−.2085	.0382	29.8742	1	.0000	−.2153	.8118
Age	−.0341	.0067	26.1222	1	.0000	−.2003	.9665
Marital status	−.3746	.2112	3.1443	1	.0762	−.0436	.6876
Sex	.0964	.2126	.2056	1	.6502	.0000	1.1012
Constant	3.3666	.6478	27.0112	1	.0000		

1. Identify which of the coefficients differ significantly from zero. Dividing the coefficients in the column labeled B by the standard errors in the column labeled S.E. gives the z ratio, which can be interpreted with the usual z table and selected levels of significance. Squaring the ratio of the coefficient to the standard error gives chi-square values—presented as the Wald statistic in the SPSS output. Based on the chi-square distribution, the probability associated with each Wald statistic follows in another column headed "Sig."

   Education and age exceed usual significance levels, but marital status and sex do not. In addition, the natural log of the sample size used by the BIC equals 6.23 for this sample. Subtracting this value from the Wald statistic shows a very strong level of evidence for age and education. Insignificant by usual standards, marital status and sex also fail to meet the BIC for significance.

2. Interpret the meaning and direction of the coefficients for each variable in the equation in terms of logged odds. The coefficients show that a 1-year increase in age lowers the logged odds of smoking by .034; a 1-year increase in education lowers the logged odds of smoking by .208; the logged odds of smoking are .096 higher for females than males; and the logged odds of smoking are .375 lower for married than unmarried persons. The differences in logged odds for the categories of sex and marital status likely do not differ from zero in the population, but I interpret them for the purposes of illustration.

3. For the continuous independent variables, translate the coefficients into effects on the odds of smoking. The SPSS output lists each coefficient as an exponent in the last column. Subtracting one from each exponentiated coefficient and multiplying by 100 shows the percentage change in the odds of smoking for a one-unit change in X:

   > Education: A 1-year increase in education reduces the odds by a multiple of .812, or by 18.8% (since $(.812 - 1) * 100 = -18.8$).
   >
   > Age: A 1-year increase in age reduces the odds by a multiple of .966 or by 3.40% (since $(.966 - 1) * 100 = -3.40$).

Although both education and age are measured in years, the ranges and standard deviations of the two variables differ. To make the coefficients more comparable, it helps to calculate the percentage change in odds for a one standard deviation change. For education, multiply the standard deviation of 3.09 by the logistic regression coefficient of $-.2085$, and then find the exponential of the product. The resulting coefficient of .525 shows that a standard deviation unit increase in education reduces the odds of smoking by 47.5% $((.525 - 1) * 100)$. For age, the standard deviation of 17.38 and the logistic regression coefficient of $-.0341$ yields an exponentiated coefficient of .553; a standard unit increase in age thus reduces the odds of smoking by 44.7%. Although not fully standardized, these coefficients reveal that the two variables have similar effects.

4. For the dummy variable groups, compare the odds of smoking. In the first case, the comparison involves married relative to unmarried persons, and in the second case involves females relative to males. The exponentiated logistic regression coefficients for the dummy variables show:

> Marital Status: The odds are $(.688 - 1) * 100$ or 31.2% lower for married than unmarried persons.
> Sex: The odds are $(1.10 - 1) * 100$ or 10.0% higher for females than males.

The exponentiated coefficients also represent the odds ratios of married to unmarried persons and females to males. The odds of smoking for married persons as a ratio to the odds for unmarried persons equal .688; the odds of smoking are 31 percent lower for married than unmarried persons. The odds ratio of females to males equals 1.10; the odds of smoking are 10 percent higher for females than males.

5. Calculate the marginal effect of the continuous independent variables on the probability of smoking at the sample mean. With the proportion smoking equal to .276, use the formula for the partial derivative:

> Education: $-.2085 * .276 * .724 = -.042$. A 1-year increase in education reduces the probability of smoking by .042 or 4.2% at the mean probability.
> Age: $-.0341 * .276 * .724 = -.007$. A 1-year increase in age reduces the probability of smoking by .007 or 0.7% at the mean probability.

6. Calculate the differences in predicted probabilities for the dummy variable groups at the sample mean. The mean proportion smoking of .276 equals a logit of $-.964$.

> Marital Status: The predicted logit for married persons equals $-.964 - .3746 = -1.339$, which gives a probability of .208; married persons thus have a .068 lower probability of smoking than unmarried persons $(.208 - .276 = -.068)$ at the sample mean.
> Sex: The predicted logit for females equals $-.964 + .0964 = -.8676$, which gives a probability of .296; females thus have a .020 higher probability of smoking than males $(.296 - .276 = .020)$ at the sample mean.

7. Calculate the differences in predicted probabilities for a one-unit change in education and age at the mean proportion smoking of .276. Again, the logit of the mean proportion smoking equals −.964. Add the logistic regression coefficient to this logit and then find the probability.[11]

Education: −.964 − .2085 = −1.1725, which gives a probability of .236; a 1-year increase in education lowers the predicted probability of smoking by .04 (.236 − .276 = −.040).
Age: −.964 − .0341 = −.9981, which gives a probability of .269; a 1-year increase in age lowers the predicted probability of smoking by .007 (.269 − .276 = −.007).

8. Compute standardized coefficients for the independent variables. SPSS saves the predicted probabilities from logistic regression. The predicted probabilities for smoking have a correlation with the observed dummy dependent variable of .319 and a correlation squared (i.e., variance explained in the dependent variable by the independent variables) of .1018. Once transformed back into logits, the predicted values have a variance of .6195. Following Menard, the variance of Y equals the variance of the predicted logits divided by the variance explained, and the standard deviation equals the square root of this ratio:

$$s_y^2 = .6195/.1018 = 6.085, \quad \text{and} \quad s_y = 2.467.$$

Following Long, the variance of Y equals the variance of the predicted logits plus the variance of the logistic distribution:

$$s_y^2 = .6195 + 3.290 = 3.909, \quad \text{and} \quad s_y = 1.977.$$

Using the formula for standardized coefficients, Table 2.2 makes the calculations. One method gives larger standardized coefficients than the other method, but both indicate that education and age have the strongest influence on smoking.

TABLE 2.2

			Menard		Long	
	b	S_x	S_y	B^*	S_y	B^*
Education	−.2085	3.09	2.467	−.261	1.977	−.326
Age	−.0341	17.38	2.467	−.240	1.977	−.300
Marital status	−.3746	.4985	2.467	−.076	1.977	−.094
Sex	.0964	.4977	2.467	.019	1.977	.024

Summary

Logistic regression coefficients provide a simple linear and additive summary of the influence of a variable on the logged odds of having a characteristic or experiencing an event, but lack an intuitively meaningful scale of interpretation of change in the dependent variable. Raising e to the coefficient b allows interpretation of the resulting coefficient in terms of multiplicative odds or percentage change in the odds. Various procedures also exist to calculate the effects of independent variables on the probability of having a characteristic or experiencing an event. However, effects on probabilities depend on the point of the logistic curve at which the effect is calculated. Although the mean of the dependent variable supplies a reasonable point for the calculation, the inherently nonlinear and nonadditive relationship between independent variables and probabilities makes this approach controversial. Standard tests of significance offer another common way to interpret the results, but by themselves say little about the substantive meaning of the coefficients. Calculating standardized coefficients may also help, but different methods of calculation can give different figures.

3. ESTIMATION AND MODEL FIT

The last chapter treated logistic regression coefficients as similar to ordinary regression coefficients, only based on a nonlinear and nonadditive transformation of the dependent variable from probabilities to logits. In so doing, the discussion focused on the predicted probabilities of experiencing an event or having a characteristic for either individual cases or sets of values on the independent variables. However, data on individuals usually include values of only 0 and 1 for the dependent variable rather than the actual probabilities. Without known probabilities, the estimation procedure must use observed values of 0 and 1 on dummy dependent variables to obtain predicted probabilities.

As discussed earlier, the dichotomous dependent variable makes estimation using ordinary least squares inappropriate. The error term has neither a normal distribution nor equal variances for values of the independent variables. Therefore, the estimation procedure derived from the least squares criterion—minimizing the sum of the squared deviations between the observed and predicted values of the dependent variable—no longer gives efficient estimates.

Instead of least squares, logistic regression relies on maximum likelihood procedures to obtain the coefficient estimates. As a general and flexible strategy, maximum likelihood estimation applies to a variety of models (Eliason, 1993), but this chapter illustrates the logic of the estimation technique for logistic regression. Relying on simple terms and examples, the chapter highlights the differences and similarities between least squares concepts used in ordinary regression and maximum likelihood concepts used in logistic regression. Although not essential for interpreting logistic regression coefficients, some knowledge of estimation procedures helps to explain the source of common hypothesis tests and measures of model accuracy. The last part of the chapter thus extends the discussion of estimation to consider these topics.

Maximum Likelihood Estimation

Maximum likelihood estimation finds estimates of model parameters that are most likely to give rise to the pattern of observations in the sample data. To illustrate the maximum likelihood principle, consider a simple example involving tossing a coin. Suppose a coin tossed 10 times gives 4 heads and 6 tails. Letting P equal the probability of a head and $1 - P$ the probability of a tail, the probability of obtaining 4 heads and 6 tails equals:

$$P(4 \text{ heads, 6 tails}) = 10!/4!6!\left[P^4 * (1 - P)^6\right].$$

We might normally assume that, with a fair coin, P equals .5 and compute the probability of obtaining four heads. If P is unknown and we need to evaluate the coin's fairness, however, the question becomes: how can P be estimated from the observed outcome of 4 heads over 10 tosses? Maximum likelihood estimation chooses the P that makes the probability of getting the observed outcome as large as possible.

In finding the maximum likelihood estimate of P, we can focus on the $P^4 * (1 - P)^6$ component of the preceding formula. This formula expresses the likelihood of obtaining four heads as a function of varied values of P. Substituting possible values of P into the likelihood function gives the results in Table 3.1. It appears that the maximum value occurs when P equals .4.[12] Further checking the likelihood using the same formula when P varies from .35 to .45 confirms that .4 produces the maximum likelihood. Given the data, the most likely or maximum likelihood estimate of P equals .4. In this way, we pick as the parameter estimate for P the value that gives the highest likelihood of producing the actual observations.

For logistic regression, the procedure begins with an expression for the likelihood of observing the pattern of occurrences ($Y = 1$) and nonoccurrences ($Y = 0$) of an event or characteristic in a given sample. This expression, termed the likelihood function, depends on unknown logistic regression parameters. As in the coin tossing example, maximum likelihood estimation finds the model parameters that give the maximum value for the likelihood function. It thereby identifies the estimates for model parameters that are most likely to give rise to the pattern of observations in the sample data.

The maximum likelihood function in logistic regression parallels the previous formula:

$$LF = \prod \left\{ P_i^{Y_i} * (1 - P_i)^{1-Y_i} \right\},$$

where LF refers to the likelihood, Y_i refers to the observed value of the dichotomous dependent variable for case i, and P_i refers to the predicted probability for case i. Recall that the P_i values come from a logistic regression model and the formula $P_i = 1/(1 + e^{-L_i})$, where L_i equals the logged odds determined by the unknown parameters β and the independent variables. $\prod$ refers to the multiplicative equivalent of the summation sign, and means that the function multiplies the values for each case. The key is to identify β values that produce L_i and P_i values that maximize LF.

Consider how this formula works. For a case in which Y_i equals 1, the formula reduces to P_i because P_i raised to the power 1 equals P_i,

TABLE 3.1

P	$P^4 * (1 - P)^6$	P	$P^4 * (1 - P)^6$	P	$P^4 * (1 - P)^6$
.1	.0000531	.4	.0011944	.7	.0001750
.2	.0004194	.5	.0009766	.8	.0000262
.3	.0009530	.6	.0005308	.9	.0000007

and $(1 - P_i)$ raised to the power zero $(1 - Y_i)$ equals 1. Thus, when $Y_i = 1$ the value for a case equals its predicted probability. If, based on the model coefficients, the case has a high predicted probability of the occurrence of an event when $Y_i = 1$, it contributes more to the likelihood than if it has a low probability of the occurrence of an event.

For a case in which Y_i equals 0, the formula reduces to $1 - P_i$ because P_i raised to the power 0 equals 1 while $(1 - P_i)$ raised to the power 1 equals $1 - P_i$. Thus, when $Y_i = 0$ the value for a case equals 1 minus its predicted probability. If the case has a low predicted probability of the occurrence of an event based on the model coefficients when $Y_i = 0$, it contributes more to the likelihood than if it has a high probability (e.g., if $P_i = .1$, then $1 - P_i = .9$, which counts more than if $P_i = .9$ and $1 - P_i = .1$).

Take, for example, four cases. Two have scores of 1 on the dependent variable, and two have scores of 0. Assume that the estimated coefficients in combination with the values of the independent variables produce the predicted probabilities for each of the four cases listed in Table 3.2. Using the probabilities with the formula gives the results for each case in Table 3.2. For each case, the final value indicates the likelihood of the observation given the estimated coefficients; in this example, the observations have relatively high likelihoods. Compare these results to another set of estimated coefficients that in combination with the values of X produce different predicted probabilities and results for the likelihood formula (see Table 3.3). Here, the estimated coefficients do worse in producing the actual Y values, and the likelihood values are lower.

Given a set of estimates for the models parameters, then, the maximum likelihood function returns for each case a probability of actually observing the sample values. Multiplying these probabilities gives a summary indication over all cases of the likelihood that a set of coefficients produces the actual values. Multiplying probabilities means

TABLE 3.2

Y_i	P_i	$P_i^{Y_i}$	$(1 - P_i)^{1-Y_i}$	$P_i^{Y_i} * (1 - P_i)^{1-Y_i}$
1	.8	$.8^1 = .8$	$.2^0 = 1$	.8
1	.7	$.7^1 = .7$	$.3^0 = 1$	.7
0	.3	$.3^0 = 1$	$.7^1 = .7$	.7
0	.2	$.2^0 = 1$	$.8^1 = .8$	.8

TABLE 3.3

Y_i	P_i	$P_i^{Y_i}$	$(1 - P_i)^{1-Y_i}$	$P_i^{Y_i} * (1 - P_i)^{1-Y_i}$
1	.2	$.2^1 = .2$	$.2^0 = 1$	.2
1	.3	$.3^1 = .3$	$.3^0 = 1$	.3
0	.7	$.3^0 = 1$	$.3^1 = .3$	.3
0	.8	$.2^0 = 1$	$.2^1 = .3$	.2

that the total product cannot exceed one or fall below zero. It will equal one in the unlikely event that every case with a 1 has a predicted value of 1 and every case with a 0 has a predicted value of 0. This likelihood equals .8*.7*.7*.8 or .3136 for the first set of coefficients, and .2*.3.*3*.2 or .0036 for the second. What is already obvious from the more detailed results shows in a single number. The hypothetical coefficients in the first example give a larger likelihood function value than the second, and are more likely to have given rise to the observed data.

Log Likelihood Function

To avoid multiplication of probabilities (and typically having to deal with exceedingly small numbers), the likelihood function can be turned into a logged likelihood function. Since

$$\ln(X * Y) = \ln X + \ln Y,$$

and

$$\ln(X^Z) = Z * \ln X,$$

the log likelihood function sums the formerly multiplicative terms. Taking the natural log of both sides of the likelihood equation gives the log likelihood function:

$$\ln LF = \sum \left\{ [Y_i * \ln P_i] + [(1 - Y_i) * \ln(1 - P_i)] \right\}.$$

If the likelihood function varies between 0 and 1, the log likelihood function will vary from negative infinity to zero (the natural log of 1 equals 0, and the natural log of 0 is undefined, but as the probability gets closer to zero the natural log becomes an increasing negative

TABLE 3.4

Y_i	P_i	$Y_i * \ln P_i$	$(1 - Y_i) * \ln(1 - P_i)$	$[Y_i * \ln P_i] + [(1 - Y_i) * \ln(1 - P_i)]$
1	.8	$1 * -.223$	$0 * -1.609$	$-.223$
1	.7	$1 * -.357$	$0 * -1.204$	$-.357$
0	.3	$0 * -1.204$	$1 * -.357$	$-.357$
0	.2	$0 * -1.609$	$1 * -.223$	$-.223$

number). The closer the likelihood value is to 1, then the closer the log likelihood value is to 0, and the more likely it is that the parameters could produce the observed data. The more distant the negative value from zero, the less likely that the parameters could produce the observed data.

To illustrate the log likelihood function, we can go through the same examples that appear earlier. In Table 3.4, the sum equals -1.16. The same calculation for the second set of coefficients appears in Table 3.5. The sum equals -5.626. Again, coefficients that best produce the observed values show a higher value (i.e., smaller negative number) for the log likelihood function.

Estimation

Maximum likelihood estimation aims to find those coefficients that have the greatest likelihood of producing the observed data. In practice, this means maximizing the log likelihood function. Hypothetically, we could proceed in a bivariate model something like this.

1. Pick coefficients for the parameters, say, for example, 1 and .3 in a bivariate model.
2. For the first case multiply b by the X value and add the product to the constant to get a predicted logit (if X equals 2 for the first case, the predicted logit equals $1 + 2 * .3 = 1.6$).

TABLE 3.5

Y_i	P_i	$Y_i * \ln P_i$	$(1 - Y_i) * \ln(1 - P_i)$	$[Y_i * \ln P_i] + [(1 - Y_i) * \ln(1 - P_i)]$
1	.2	$1 * -1.609$	$0 * -.223$	-1.609
1	.3	$1 * -1.204$	$0 * -.357$	-1.204
0	.7	$0 * -.357$	$1 * -1.204$	-1.204
0	.8	$0 * -.223$	$1 * -1.609$	-1.609

3. Translate the logit into a probability using the formula

$$P = 1/1 + e^{-L} = e^{L}/1 + e^{L}.$$

For the first case, the probability equals $1/1 + e^{-1.6} = 1/1 + .2019 = .832$.

4. If $Y = 1$, then the contribution to the log likelihood function for this case equals $1 * \ln .832 + 0 * \ln .168 = -.1839$.

5. Repeat steps 1–4 for each of the other cases, and sum the components of the log likelihood function to get a total value.

6. Repeat the steps for another pair of coefficients, and compare the log likelihood value to that for the first set of coefficients.

7. Do this for all possible coefficients and pick the ones that generate the largest log likelihood value (i.e., closest to zero).

Of course, mathematical formulas and computing procedures allow logistic regression programs to more efficiently identify the estimates that maximize the log likelihood function. A program usually begins with a model in which all b coefficients equal the least squares estimates. It then uses an algorithm to successively choose new sets of coefficients that produce larger log likelihoods and better fit with the observed data. It continues through the iterations or cycles of this process until the increase in the log likelihood function from choosing new parameters becomes so small (and the coefficients change so little) that little benefit comes from continuing any further.

Tests of Significance Using Log Likelihood Values

The log likelihood value reflects the likelihood that the data would be observed given the parameter estimates. It can be thought of as the deviation from a perfect or saturated model in which the log likelihood equals 0. The larger the value (i.e., the closer the negative value to zero), the better the parameters do in producing the observed data. Although it increases with the effectiveness of the parameters, the log likelihood value has little intuitive meaning because it depends on the sample size and number of parameters as well as on the goodness of fit. We therefore need a standard to help evaluate its relative size.

One way to interpret the size of the log likelihood involves comparing the model value to the initial or baseline value assuming all the b coefficients equal zero. The baseline log likelihood comes from including only a constant term in the model—the equivalent of using the mean probability as the predicted value for all cases. The greater the difference between the baseline log likelihood and the model log likelihood, the better the model coefficients (along with the independent variables) do in producing the observed sample values. This difference can be used in hypothesis testing (as well as in measures of goodness of fit discussed shortly). Like the F test in regression, the difference in the baseline and model log likelihood values evaluates the null hypothesis that $b_1 = b_2 = \cdots = b_k = 0$. It does so by determining if the difference is larger than would be expected from random error alone.

The test proceeds as follows. Take the difference between the baseline log likelihood and the model log likelihood. Multiplying that difference by -2 gives a chi-square value with degrees of freedom equal to the number of independent variables (not including the constant, but including squared and interaction terms). Used in combination with the chi-square table, the chi-square value tests the null hypothesis that all coefficients other than the constant equal 0. It reveals if the change in the log likelihood due to all independent variables could have occurred by chance beyond a prespecified significance level (i.e., the improvement in the log likelihood does not differ significantly from zero). For a given degree of freedom, the larger the chi-square value, the greater the model improvement over the baseline, and the less likely that all the variable coefficients equal 0 in the population.

Multiplying the log likelihood difference by -2 to obtain the chi-square value is equivalent to multiplying the baseline and model log likelihood values by -2, and then taking the difference in the values to measure the model improvement. Reported either way, the results are the same. However, keep in mind that multiplying by -2 reverses the direction of the log likelihood values.

Using the four cases presented earlier illustrates this significance test. Without knowledge of X, the baseline model would use the mean of Y, say .5, as the predicted probability for each case. Using the likelihood and log likelihood functions, and substituting predicted probabilities of .5 for each case, gives a likelihood of .0625 and a log likelihood of -2.773 for the baseline model. If X relates to Y, however, the log likelihood knowing X should be closer to zero and reflect a better model than the log likelihood not knowing X. Assume that the log likelihood value computed earlier is maximum. It has a likelihood value of .3136 and a log likelihood value of -1.160. A summary comparison of the baseline and final models in Table 3.6 shows the improvement from knowing X.

TABLE 3.6

Model	LF	LLF	−2(LLF)
Baseline model	.0625	−2.773	5.546
Final model	.3136	−1.160	2.320
Difference	−.2511	−1.613	3.226

Although the units of these figures make little intuitive sense, one can see improvement in the final model compared to the initial or baseline model. A test of significance using the chi-square distribution tells if the 3.226 improvement likely could have occurred by chance alone (at a preselected probability level). With 1 degree of freedom for the one independent variable, the critical chi-square value at .05 equals 3.8414. Since the actual chi-square does not reach the critical value, we can conclude that the independent variable does not significantly influence the dependent variable. Of course, this artificial example with only four cases makes it difficult to reach any level of statistical significance, but it illustrates the use of the chi-square test.

In review, then, the likelihood values range from 0 to 1, while the log likelihood values range from negative infinity to zero. The baseline model typically shows lower likelihood and log likelihood values than the final model. The larger the likelihood and log likelihood values for the final model are relative to the baseline model values, the greater the improvement from estimating nonzero parameters. The log likelihood values times −2, which range from 0 to positive infinity, reverse the direction of interpretation to be more in line with common interpretations of the error in regression models. Because it typically performs worse in reproducing the observed data, the baseline model now shows a higher value than the final model. Again, however, the larger the difference between the two models, the larger the improvement in the model due to the independent variables.

Often times researchers refer to the chi-square difference or the improvement in the log likelihood as the likelihood ratio. The log of the ratio of the baseline likelihood to the model likelihood equals the difference between the two log likelihoods. The general principle is that

$$\ln X - \ln Y = \ln(X/Y).$$

In the example, the ratio of the likelihood values divides .0625 by .3136. The log of this value equals −1.613, which is identical to the difference in the log likelihood values. Multiplying the likelihood ratio by -2 gives the chi-square value for the test of the overall model significance.

The same logic of the chi-square test of the difference between the baseline and the final models applies to the comparison of any two nested models. If a full model contains k (e.g., 10) variables, and a restricted model contains h fewer variables than the full model (e.g., 6 fewer or 4 total), the chi-square can test the null hypothesis that the coefficients for the h variables added to the restricted model all equal zero. Simply subtract the log likelihood of the full model from the log likelihood of the restricted model and multiply that result by -2. Equivalently, subtract -2 times the log likelihood for the full model from -2 times the log likelihood for the restricted model. In both cases, the result equals a chi-square value with h degrees of freedom. The test of the baseline model represents a sub-case of the more general nested model where h includes all variables in the full model.

This procedure can test for the significance of a single variable by comparing equations with and without the variable in question (i.e., h refers to one variable). Subtracting -2 times the log likelihood for the model with the variable from -2 times the log likelihood for the model without the variable provides a chi-square statistic for the individual variable; the test can in certain instances give more precise values than the Wald test discussed in the last chapter (Long, 1997, pp. 97–98).

Model Evaluation

Although the dependent variable in logistic regression does not have variance in the same way continuous variables do in regression, maximum likelihood procedures provide model fit measures analogous to those from least squares regression. As in tests of significance, it makes intuitive sense to compare a model knowing the independent variables to a model not knowing them. In regression, the total sum of squares follows from a model not knowing the independent variables, the error sum of squares follows from a model knowing the independent variables, and the difference indicates the improvement due to the independent variables. In logistic regression, the baseline log likelihood ($L0$) times -2 represents the likelihood of producing the observed data with parameters for the independent variables equaling zero, and corresponds to the total sum of squares. The model log likelihood ($L1$) times -2 represents the likelihood of producing the observed data with the estimated parameters for the independent variables, and corresponds to the error sum of squares in regression. The improvement relative to the baseline in the log likelihood model shows the improvement due to the independent variables. Accordingly, these two log likelihoods define an analogy to a proportional reduction-in-error measure in regression[13]:

$$R^2 = [(-2\ln L0) - (-2\ln L1)]/(-2\ln L0).$$

The numerator shows the reduction in the model "error" due to the independent variables, and the denominator shows the "error" without using the independent variables. The resulting value shows the improvement in the log likelihood relative to the baseline. It equals 0 when all the coefficients equal 0, and has a maximum that comes close to 1.[14] However, the measure does not represent explained variance since log likelihood functions do not deal with variance defined as the sum of squared deviations. This and similar measures are therefore referred to as the pseudo-variance explained or pseudo R^2.

Another measure builds on the fact that the log likelihood value depends on the number of cases. Consequently, the chi-square value due to the independent variables (or improvement in -2 times the log likelihood in the numerator of the previous equation) can be taken as a proportion of the chi-square plus the sample size. Aldrich and Nelson (1984) thus present the following measure of the pseudo-variance explained:

$$R^2 = \chi^2/(\chi^2 + N).$$

This measure does not under most circumstances have a maximum of 1. Hagle and Mitchell (1992) demonstrate that the maximum value depends on the percentage of cases in the largest category of the dependent variable. They also list a set of multiples defined by the percentage of cases in the largest category that corrects the Aldrich and Nelson measure.[15] The corrected measure will have a minimum of 0 and maximum of 1 and performs well as a measure of the performance of the model.

Another measure parallels the variance explained measure in regression. The multiple R in regression equals the correlation between the observed and predicted values of the dependent variable, and the R^2 equals that correlation squared. The same logic applies to logistic regression: the correlation between the observed dummy dependent variable and probabilities predicted by the logistic regression model measures the goodness of fit. Although logistic regression programs do not routinely calculate R and R^2 as they do for regression, saving predicted probabilities from logistic regression makes for easy calculation. Simply correlate the saved variable with the original dummy variable after doing the logistic regression and then square the value.

Analysts have suggested numerous other measures to assess the model. McKelvey and Zavoina (1975) use the variance of the predicted logits to define a measure of the pseudo-variance explained. Cox and Snell (1989) raise the ratio of the likelihood values to the power $2/n$ to get another measure. In addition, Nagelkerke (1991) suggests an adjustment to the Cox and Snell measure to ensure a maximum of 1. Long (1997, pp. 104–113) reviews these and several other measures that appear in the literature on logistic regression.

In summary, no consensus has emerged on the single best measure, and each measure may give different results. Researchers should use these measures as only rough guides without attributing great importance to a precise figure. In fact, many published articles using logistic regression do not present a measure of the pseudo-variance explained. Still, used carefully, measures of goodness of fit that vary from 0 to 1 can be helpful.

Another approach to model evaluation compares predicted *group membership* with observed group membership. Using the predicted probabilities for each case, logistic regression programs also predict the expected group membership. Based on a typical cut value of .5, those cases with predicted probabilities at .5 or above are predicted to score 1 on the dependent variable and those cases with predicted probabilities below .5 are predicted to score 0. Cross-classifying the two categories of the observed dependent variable with the two categories of the predicted dependent variable produces a 2 × 2 table.

A highly accurate model would show that most cases fall in the cells defined by 0 on the observed and 0 on the predicted group membership and by 1 on the observed and 1 on the predicted group membership. Relatively few cases would fall into the cells defined by a mismatch of observed and predicted group membership. A simple summary measure equals the percentage of all cases in the correctly predicted cells. A perfect model would correctly predict group membership for 100% of the cases; a failed model would do no better than chance by correctly predicting 50% of the cases. The percentage of correctly predicted cases from 50 to 100 provides a crude measure of predictive accuracy.

However, if one category of the dependent variable is substantially larger than the other, a model can do better than 50% by simply predicting the largest category for all cases. A more accurate measure takes the percentage of correctly predicted cases beyond the percentage that would be predicted by choosing the percentage in the largest category of the dependent variable (Long, 1997, pp. 107–108). Other measures of association for nominal and ordinal variables can also summarize the strength of the relationship between predicted and observed values. Menard (1995) discusses numerous measures of relationship strength for tabular data such as ϕ, τ, γ and λ. However, because the focus on predicting group membership differs from the focus on model fit, results for predictive accuracy can differ substantially from results for model fit. Further, Greene (1933, p. 652) identifies several illogical results that can emerge from the use of measures of predictive accuracy. Other than an occasional listing of percent correctly predicted, few articles report more detail on the cross-classification of observed and predicted group membership.

An Example

Table 3.7 presents selected SPSS output from the logistic regression of smoking on education, age, marital status, and sex. The information in Table 3.7 relates to issues of general model fit, and precedes the coefficient estimates from the SPSS output shown in Table 2.1.

1. Compare −2 times the baseline log likelihood with −2 times the model log likelihood. The beginning block number 0 shows the initial or baseline log likelihood function (i.e., one that includes only a constant in the model). This log likelihood times −2 equals 601.38073, but has little meaning by itself. After entering four variables in step 1, the es-

52

TABLE 3.7
Partial SPSS Logistic Regression Output: Model Fit

Dependent variable... DSMOKE
Beginning block number   0.   Initial log likelihood function

−2 Log likelihood   601.38073

* Constant is included in the model.

Beginning block number   1. Method: Enter

Variable(s) entered on step number 1

   Education
   Age
   Marital status
   Sex

Estimation terminated at iteration number 4 because
log likelihood decreased by less than .01%

−2 Log likelihood   544.830
Goodness of fit   491.832
Cox & Snell—R^2 .105
Nagelkerke—R^2 .152

	Chi-Square	df	Significance
Model	56.551	4	.0000
Block	56.551	4	.0000
Step	56.551	4	.0000

Classification table for DSMOKE
The cut value is .50

	Predicted		
	0	1	Percent correct
Observed			
.00	349	20	94.58
1.00	112	29	20.57
		Overall	74.12

timation terminates after four iterations because the log likelihood improves by less than the default of .01%. Given the estimates, the model log likelihood function times −2 equals 544.830. The decrease in these values or improvement in the model is 56.551. As presented in the output, this chi-square value meets standard levels of significance with 4 degrees of freedom.

2. Evaluate the goodness of fit of the model. The SPSS output computes two measures of the pseudo-variance explained. The Cox and Snell measure equals .105 and the Nagelkerke adjustment raises the measure to .152. The proportional improvement in the chi-square measure equals:

$$\text{pseudo } R^2 = (601.38 - 544.83)/601.38 = 56.55/601.38$$
$$= .0940 \text{ or } 9.40\%.$$

The Aldrich and Nelson measure based on the chi-square and sample size equals:

$$\text{pseudo } R^2 = 56.551/(56.551 + 510) = .0998 = 9.98\%.$$

The correction suggested by Hagle and Mitchell (1992) uses the modal category of not smoking of 72% and a multiplier of 1.84 to obtain

$$\text{pseudo } R^2 = .0998 * 1.84 = .1836.$$

Like the Nagelkerke measure, this adjustment raises the coefficient substantially, and balances the tendency of the other measures to underestimate the model strength. Finally, saving the predicted probabilities and correlating them with the observed dependent variable gives an R of .319 and R^2 of .102 or 10.2%.

3. Evaluate the predictive accuracy. The output table cross-classifies observed by predicted group membership and reveals that the model correctly predicts 74% of the cases. However, relative to the 72% of the cases in the nonsmoking category, the 74% figure represents a small improvement.

Summary

For those familiar with ordinary regression, logistic regression provides analogs to commonly used statistics. Rather than choosing parameters that minimize the sum of squared errors, estimation in logistic regression chooses parameters that maximize the likelihood of observing sample values. Since translating familiar terms to the unfamiliar terms will make logistic regression easier to understand, the columns in Table 3.8 summarize the correspondence between ordinary and logistic regression terms.

54

TABLE 3.8

Ordinary Regression	Logistic Regression
Total sum of squares	Baseline log likelihood times −2
Error sum of squares	Model log likelihood times −2
Regression sum of squares	Difference between baseline and model log likelihoods times −2
F test for model	Chi-square for log likelihood difference
Variance explained	Pseudo-variance explained

4. PROBIT ANALYSIS

Logistic regression deals with the ceiling and floor problems in modeling a dichotomous dependent variable by transforming probabilities of an event into logits. Although probabilities vary between 0 and 1, logits or the logged odds of the probabilities have no such limits—they vary from negative to positive infinity. Many other transformations also eliminate the ceiling and floor of probabilities. Aldrich and Nelson (1984, p. 33) describe a number of S-shaped curves that differ in how rapidly or slowly the tails approach 0 and 1. The logit transformation used in logistic regression has the advantage of relative simplicity, and finds use most commonly. One other familiar transformation based on the normal curve, however, appears often in the published literature.

Another Way to Linearize the Nonlinear

Probit analysis transforms probabilities of an event into scores from the cumulative standard normal distribution rather than into logged odds from the logistic distribution. Despite this difference, probit analysis and logistic regression give essentially equivalent results, making the choice between them one of individual preferences and computer program availability. Indeed, many texts introduce logit and probit analysis simultaneously to emphasize their similarities. This chapter examines probit analysis separately, but, to also emphasize similarities, uses the earlier material on logistic regression to explain the logic of probit analysis.

To transform probabilities with a floor of 0 and a ceiling of 1 into scores without these boundaries, the probit transformation relates the probability of experiencing an event or having a characteristic to the cumulative standard normal distribution rather than to the logged odds. To explain this transformation, it helps to review the information contained in tables from any statistics text on areas of the standard normal curve. The tables match z scores (theoretically ranging from negative infinity to positive infinity, but in practice from -3 to 3) with a proportion of the area under the curve between the absolute value of the z score and the mean z score of 0. With some simple calculations, the standard normal table also identifies the proportion of the area from negative infinity to the z score. The proportion of the curve at or below each of the z scores defines the cumulative standard normal distribution. Since the proportion equals the probability that a standard normal random variable will fall at or below that z score, larger z scores define greater probabilities in the cumulative standard normal distribution.

Conversely, just as any z score defines a probability in the cumulative standard normal distribution, any probability in the cumulative standard normal distribution translates into a z score. The greater the cumulative probability, the higher the associated z score. Further, because probabilities vary between 0 and 1, and the corresponding z scores vary between positive and negative infinity, it suggests using the areas defined by the standard normal curve to transform bounded probabilities into unbounded z scores.

To illustrate, Figures 4.1 and 4.2 depict the standard normal curve and the cumulative standard normal curve. The normal curve in Figure 4.1 plots the height or density on the vertical axis for each z score on the horizontal axis, which approximates the probability of a single z value. In addition, each z score implicitly divides the curve into two portions—the portion between negative infinity and the z score, and the portion beyond the z score or between the z score and positive infinity. If the former area under the curve equals P, the latter area under the curve equals $1 - P$. Note also that the height of the normal curve drops fastest around values near 0, and changes little at the tails of the curve. Thus, P and $1 - P$ change more near the middle of the curve than near the extremes.

The cumulative standard normal curve in Figure 4.2 directly plots the area in the standard normal curve at or below each z score. As the z scores get larger, the cumulative proportion of the normal curve at or below the z score increases. As for the standard normal curve, the z scores define the X axis, but the Y axis refers to the proportion of area at or below that z score rather than to the height of the normal

56

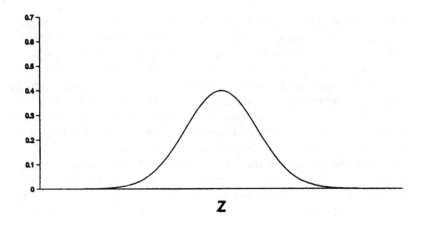

Figure 4.1. Standard normal curve.

curve. Drawing a line up to the curve from a z score, and then drawing another perpendicular line across to the Y axis, shows the cumulative probability associated with each z score and the area of the standard normal curve at or below that z score.

The cumulative standard normal curve resembles the logistic curve, only with z scores instead of logged odds along the horizontal axis. The curve approaches, but does not reach 0 as the z scores de-

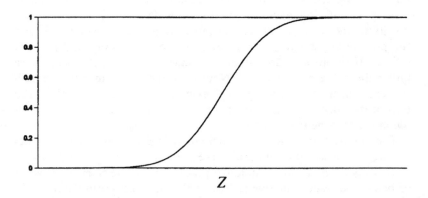

Figure 4.2. Cumulative standard normal curve.

crease toward negative infinity, and the curve approaches but does not reach 1 as the z scores increase toward positive infinity. Although the probit curve approaches the floor and ceiling slightly faster than the logit curve, the differences are small. Thus, as logistic regression uses the logistic curve to translate probabilities into logits or logged odds, probit analysis uses the cumulative standard normal curve to translate probabilities into associated z scores. Although related nonlinearly to the probabilities, independent variables relate linearly to the z scores from the probit transformation.

To illustrate the properties of the transformation used in probit analysis, the numbers below match z scores with probabilities. The first row lists z scores, and the second row lists the associated probabilities of the cumulative standard normal distribution (i.e., the area of the normal curve between negative infinity and the z score),

-4	-3	-2	-1	0	1	2	3	4
0.00003	0.00135	0.0228	0.1587	0.5	0.8413	0.9772	0.99865	0.99997.

Note the nonlinear relationship between the z scores and probabilities: the same one-unit change in the z scores produces a smaller change in the probabilities near the floor of 0 and near the ceiling of 1 than in the middle. Conversely, the probabilities in the first row below define z scores in the second row,

0.1	0.2	0.3	0.4	0.5	0.6	0.7	0.8	0.9
-1.282	-0.842	-0.524	-0.253	0	0.253	0.524	0.842	1.282.

These figures likewise show nonlinearity: the same change in probabilities results in a bigger change in z scores as the probabilities approach 0 and 1.

These examples show that the probit transformation has the same properties of the logit transformation. It has no upper or lower boundary, as the domain of the normal curve extends to infinity in either direction. It is symmetric around the midpoint probability of .5; the z scores for probabilities .4 and .6 are identical except for the sign. Additionally, the same change in probabilities translates into larger changes in z scores for probabilities near 0 and 1. The transformation thus stretches the probabilities near the boundaries. In short, translating probabilities into z scores based on the cumulative standard normal curve has the characteristics necessary to linearize certain types of nonlinear relationships.

Probit Analysis

Like logistic regression, probit analysis relies on a transformation to make regression on a dichotomous dependent variable similar to regression on a continuous variable. Given a probability of experiencing an event or having a characteristic, the predicted probit becomes the dependent variable in a linear equation determined by one or more independent variables:

$$Z_i = b_0 + b_1 * X_i.$$

Z represents the nonlinear transformation of probabilities into z scores using the cumulative standard normal distribution. By predicting the z scores with a linear equation, probit analysis implicitly describes a nonlinear relationship with probabilities in which the independent variable has a greater effect on the probabilities near the middle of the curve than near the extremes.

In logistic regression, we can summarize the transformation of probabilities into logged odds and vice-versa with relatively simple formulas. For probit analysis, the complex formula for the standard normal curve makes for more difficulty. Corresponding to the nonlinear equation for determining probabilities in logistic regression, $P_i = 1/(1 + e^{-L_i})$, the nonlinear equation for probit analysis takes P_i as a function of Z_i in the formula for the cumulative standard normal distribution. The formula involves an integral (roughly similar to summation for a continuous distribution) that transforms z scores from negative to positive infinity into probabilities with a minimum of 0 and maximum of 1. Based on the cumulative standard normal distribution, the cumulative probability associated with any z score equals:

$$P = \int_{-\infty}^{Z} \frac{1}{\sqrt{2\pi}} \exp -(U^2/2) \, dU,$$

where U is a random variable with a mean of 0 and standard deviation of 1. The formula merely says that the probability of the event equals the area under the cumulative normal curve between negative infinity and Z. The larger the value Z, the larger the cumulative probability. Because of the complexity of the formula, however, computers normally do the calculations.[16] Although hand calculators allow easy calculation of logits from probabilities and vice-versa, they seldom include functions based on the cumulative standard normal distribution. In any case, keep in mind that the goal of the formula is to translate the linearly determined Z in the probit equation back to nonlinearly determined probabilities.

Rough approximations to values generated from the formula come from the standard normal table in statistics books. For z scores from -3 to 3, the table gives the area between the mean of 0 and the absolute value of the z score. For negative z scores, subtracting the area in the table from .5 gives the area between negative infinity and the z score (i.e., defines the area of the cumulative standard normal distribution at or below that z score). For positive z scores, adding the area to .5 gives the area between negative infinity and the z score. For example, the proportion of a standard normal curve between the mean of 0 and a z score of 1.5 is .4332. Added to .5, that z score defines a probability in the cumulative standard normal curve of .9332. For a z score of -1.5, the probability in the cumulative standard normal curve equals $.5 - .4332$ or .0668.

Corresponding to the formula in logistic regression for the logged odds, $L_i = \ln(P_i/(1-P_i))$, the formula for probit analysis identifies the *inverse* of the cumulative standard normal distribution. If we represent the cumulative standard normal distribution by Φ, then the equation above equals $P = \Phi(Z)$, and the equation for Z equals $Z = \Phi^{-1}(P)$, where Φ^{-1} refers to the inverse of the cumulative standard normal distribution. Although it cannot be represented by a simple formula, the inverse of the cumulative standard normal distribution transforms probabilities into linear Z scores that represent the dependent variable in probit analysis. With probits as the dependent variable, the estimated coefficients show the change in z score units of the inverse of the cumulative standard normal distribution rather than the change in probabilities.

Finding the inverse of the cumulative standard normal distribution, or a z score from a probability, is done most easily with a computer program,[17] but using the normal table again illustrates the logic. If the probability falls below .5, then subtract it from .5 to get the area between the unknown z score and the mean of the distribution of 0. Find that area in the text of the table, and the z score associated with the area. Because the probability is less than .5, the z score will be negative. If the probability exceeds .5, then subtract .5, find the area in the table, and identify the z score associated with the probability.

A probability of .4, for example, defines an area of .10 between the z score and the mean. The z score closest to that probability in the standard normal table is 0.253. Thus, $-.253$ defines the z score in the cumulative standard normal distribution. A probability of .6 again defines an area of .10 between the z score and the mean, but this time the corresponding z score is 0.253.

Despite the similarities of the logit and probit transformations, however, the resulting coefficients differ by an arbitrary constant. The microlevel data include only the observed values of the dependent variable of 0 and 1 rather than the actual observed probabilities, and the predicted logit or probit values can range from negative to positive infinity. The logit and probit variables therefore have no inherent scale, and programs use an arbitrary normalization to fix the scale. Probit analysis sets the standard deviation of the error equal to 1, where logit analysis sets the standard deviation of the error equal to approximately 1.814.

Different error variances mean that one should not directly compare probit and logit coefficients. The logit coefficients will exceed the probit coefficients by an approximate factor of 1.8. Dividing the logit coefficients by that factor will make the units comparable,[18] but the logistic regression and probit coefficients will vary slightly because of the small differences between the logistic and normal curves. Nearly always, however, probit analysis and logistic regression produce similar substantive results.

Interpreting the Coefficients

Probit Coefficients

Given the transformed units of the dependent variable, probit coefficients warrant the usual interpretations of coefficients in regression. They show the linear and additive change in z-score units of the probit transformation (i.e., the inverse of the cumulative standard normal distribution) for a one-unit change in the independent variables. Perhaps even less intuitive than logged odds, standard units of the cumulative normal distribution have little interpretive value. By necessity, interpretations usually begin with the sign of the coefficients and the value of the t ratios. In a probit analysis of support for capital punishment using the 1993 GSS, for example, the coefficient for education equals $-.048$. A 1-year increase in education reduces the probit of the probability of supporting capital punishment by .048 units. More helpfully, the coefficient divided by its standard error equals −3.76.

An indication of the relative size of the effects within a probit equation can come from simple calculations. Multiplying the probit coefficients by the standard deviations of the independent variables would show the change in the inverse of the cumulative standard normal transformation of the dependent variable for a one standard deviation increase in the independent variable. In the example of capital punishment, education has a standard deviation of 2.984. Multiplying the standard deviation by the probit coefficient of −.048 indicates that a one standard deviation increase in education lowers support for capital punishment by −.143 probit units. Another variable measuring political views (1 = extremely liberal, 7 = extremely conservative) has a probit coefficient of .151 and a standard deviation of 1.359. The product of .205 reveals a stronger effect than for education.

Other types of standardized probit coefficients parallel those for logistic regression. Since adding the variance of the predicted logit values to the variance of the logistic error term measures the variance of the dependent variable in logistic regression, adding the variance of the predicted probit values to the variance of 1 for the probit error term suggests a probit-specific measure of variance. The square root gives a standard deviation measure of Y, and the probit coefficient multiplied by the ratio of the standard deviation of X to the standard deviation of Y yields a standardized coefficient.

Similarly, since dividing the variance of the predicted logit values by the variance explained in logistic regression offers another measure of the variance in the dependent variable, dividing the variance of the predicted probit values by the variance explained offers another measure of the variance of the dependent variable in probit analysis. After taking the square root of the variance, the standardized coefficient again comes from simple multiplication. For more details, see Chapter 2.

Otherwise, exponentiating probit coefficients does not, as it does for logistic regression coefficients, produce the equivalent of the multiplicative change in odds. Given the usefulness of multiplicative odds coefficients in logistic regression, the lack of comparable coefficients in probit analysis may contribute to the greater popularity of logistic regression. Further interpretation of probit coefficients therefore requires attention to probabilities.

Marginal Effects

The partial derivative shows the effect of an instantaneous change in an independent variable on the probability of experiencing an event or having a characteristic (i.e., the slope of the tangent line at a particular point of the nonlinear curve relating an independent variable to the probability). However, the partial derivative for probit analysis takes a different form than in logistic regression:

$$\partial P / \partial X_k = b_k * f(Z),$$

where $f(Z)$ is the density or height of the normal curve at the point Z. As shown in the next formula, the density of the standard normal curve at the value of Z differs from the formula for the area at or below a z score:

$$f(Z) = \frac{1}{\sqrt{2\pi}} \exp - (Z^2/2).$$

Given the continuous nature of the normal distribution, the probability associated with each z score is infinitely small. However, as the change in the z score approaches a limit of 0, the probability approaches the value defined by the above formula. The distribution defined by the formula has its highest value at the mean z score of 0, and has successively smaller values as the z score deviates in either direction from 0.

The formula shows that the b_k coefficients translate into the largest instantaneous effects on probabilities when the value of the normal density function is largest (i.e., when the Z value is near 0). The b_k translate into smaller effects on probabilities when the Z value is far from 0 and the density of the normal distribution is low. Values for the density of the normal curve sometimes appear in books of statistical tables, or can be calculated with hand calculators more easily than values for the cumulative standard normal distribution.[19]

Consider the probit analysis of capital punishment again. The mean of the dependent variable, .775, corresponds to a z score for the cumulative normal distribution of .755. The density of the normal curve at the z score of .755 equals .300. When multiplied by the education coefficient of −.048, the ordinate shows that the change in the probability for a 1-year change in education equals −.014. Of course, the coefficient −.048 would translate into different probabilities for different z scores. As in logistic regression, the use of a single partial derivative cannot fully summarize a complex nonlinear and nonadditive relationship. The mean probability offers only one of many possible points discussed in Chapter 2 at which to calculate marginal effects.

Effects on Predicted Probabilities

Because partial derivatives have little meaning for dummy independent variables, it helps to calculate predicted probabilities for the groups defined by a dummy variable. In addition, because the tangent line defined by the partial derivative may differ from the actual change in the probit curve for a one-unit change in a continuous independent variable, it can help to calculate the predicted change in probabilities for continuous variables. Like logistic regression, probit analysis allows calculation of changes in probabilities for specified values of the independent variables. Again, however, the effects of dummy and continuous variables on predicted probabilities depend on the choice of the starting point. Changes in probabilities will emerge larger for points near the middle of the curve than near the floor or ceiling.

To calculate the change in probabilities for a dummy variable, take the mean of the dependent variable as the predicted probability for the omitted group. Translate that value into a z score for the cumulative normal curve (i.e., the area below the z score) using a table or computer function. Then add the probit coefficient for the dummy variable to this z score and transform the new z score sum back into a new probability using a table or computer function. The new probability minus the mean shows the difference in predicted probabilities between the two groups.

For example, a dummy variable for sex (1 = female) has a coefficient in the probit equation for support of capital punishment of −.291. At the mean probability of .775, the predicted probit z score equals .755. Adding .755 to −.291 gives a probit z score of .464, and the probability associated with .464 is .677. Subtracting the probability of .775 from .677 equals −.098. At the mean of the dependent variable, the probability of women supporting capital punishment is .098 lower than for men.

The same logic of calculating predicted probabilities holds for continuous variables. After translating the mean probability into a probit z score, add the coefficient for the continuous variable and transform the probit back into a probability. The difference between the two probabilities gives the predicted change due to a one-unit change in the continuous variable. With a mean probability of .775 and probit of .755, adding the coefficient for education of $-.048$ gives a predicted probit of .707. The probability associated with .707 is .760, and the difference between probabilities is $-.015$.

The same qualifications concerning the calculations of marginal effects apply to predicted probabilities. A single coefficient cannot fully describe the relationship of a variable with probabilities, and the effect of a unit change on probabilities differs depending on the starting z score and the values of the independent variables. One can also summarize the effects of changes in the independent variables on the probabilities at the mean of all the independent variables, or at any number of other illustrative values of the independent variables.

Maximum Likelihood Estimation

Like logistic regression, probit analysis uses maximum likelihood estimation techniques. To briefly review the material in Chapter 3, maximum likelihood estimation chooses the estimates of model parameters that are most likely to give rise to the pattern of observations in the sample data. The likelihood function takes the likelihood of observing the pattern of occurrences ($Y = 1$) and nonoccurrences ($Y = 0$) of an event or characteristic in a given sample as a function of unknown model parameters. Maximizing the likelihood function therefore identifies the estimates for model parameters that are most likely to give rise to the pattern of observations in the sample data.

Probit analysis maximum likelihood estimation proceeds identically to logistic regression maximum likelihood estimation in most ways. The likelihood function, defined earlier as

$$LF = \prod \left\{ P_i^{Y_i} * (1 - P_i)^{1-Y_i} \right\},$$

reaches its largest value when the chosen probit coefficients maximize the likelihood of observing the sample values. The procedure differs from logistic regression in its use of the cumulative standard normal distribution rather than the logistic distribution to obtain P values from the independent variables and the parameter estimates. To make the computations easier, programs maximize the log likelihood function rather than the likelihood function. Since the log likelihood function produces negative values, the maximum value comes closest to 0. The estimation procedure uses an iterative method of estimation and re-estimation that proceeds until the log likelihood function fails to change by a specified (and small) amount.

Each probit model therefore produces a log likelihood value that reflects the effectiveness of the parameters in producing the observed sample values. The larger the negative value of the log likelihood, the poorer the model. Comparing the base log likelihood and the model log likelihood gives a difference score that, when multiplied by -2, produces a chi-square value that tests the null hypothesis that the coefficients for all the independent variables equal 0. Finally, the log likelihood values allow calculation of several pseudo R^2 coefficients. Again, these coefficients and tests of the overall effectiveness of the model do not differ from those for logistic regression discussed in the previous chapter.

An Example

Table 4.1 presents a probit analysis using STATA that replicates the logistic regression model for smoking presented in Chapters 2 and 3. The coefficient for education shows that for each additional year of schooling, smoking declines by .126 units of the probit transformation or the inverse of the cumulative standard normal function, and the coefficient for age shows that for a 1-year increase, smoking declines by .020 probit units. The ratios of both coefficients to their standard errors (shown in the column labeled z) exceed critical values. The coefficient for the marital status dummy variable shows married persons smoke .245 probit units less than unmarried persons, and the coefficient for the sex dummy variable shows females smoke .044 probit units more than males. The coefficient for marital status reaches the .05 level of significance, while the coefficient for sex does not.

Multiplying the coefficients for education and age by their standard deviations allows for comparison of the relative effects of the two variables. For a standard unit increase in education, the probit for smoking declines by .389; for a standard unit increase in age, the pro-

TABLE 4.1
STATA Probit Analysis Results

Iteration 0: log likelihood = −300.69036
Iteration 1: log likelihood = −272.32072
Iteration 2: log likelihood = −271.87610
Iteration 3: log likelihood = −271.87565

Probit estimates

Number of obs = 510
$\chi(4) = 57.63$
Prob > $\chi^z = 0.0000$
Pseudo $R^2 = 0.0958$

Log likelihood = −271.87565

Smokes	Coef.	Std. Err	z	P > |z|
Education	−.1258692	.0224873	−5.597	0.000
Age	−.0202936	.0038746	−5.238	0.000
Marital	−.2452985	.1246171	−1.968	0.049
Sex	.0442283	.1254098	0.353	0.724
Constant	2.034328	.3831415	5.310	0.000

bit for smoking declines by .348. These semi-standardized coefficients show a slightly stronger effect of education than age.

Calculations using the predicted probit values produce fully standardized coefficients. One measure of the variance of the dependent variable equals the variance of the predicted probit values divided by the variance explained. This value equals 2.3225 and the standard deviation equals 1.524. Another measure of the variance of the dependent variable equals the variance of the predicted probit values plus the variance of 1 for the probit distribution. This value equals 1.2383 and the standard deviation equals 1.113. The standardized coefficients for education equal, respectively, −.255 and −.350 according to the two calculations. The notable difference between the two estimates reveals the difficulties in calculating standardized coefficients. However, the standardized coefficients for age, −.231 and −.317, both reflect slightly smaller effects than education.

Differences appear in the probit and logistic regression results. Comparing Table 4.1 with Table 2.1 discloses that the logistic regression coefficients exceed the corresponding probit coefficients by a factor varying from 1.5 to 2.2. Part of the differences in coefficients result from the different variances of the transformed dependent variables. In addition, however, most z scores for the probit analysis are slightly larger than those for the logistic regression (or more precisely, than the square root of the Wald statistic). The z score for marital status in the probit analysis reaches the .05 level of significance, but does not in the logistic regression.

Probit analysis in STATA makes it easy to calculate effects on probabilities. With a simple command change, STATA computes the partial derivative for continuous variables and differences in predicted probabilities for dummy variables. By default, the program calculates the effects on probabilities when the independent variables take their mean values—a probability similar, but not identical to the mean probability on the dependent variable. Table 4.2 presents the output from this option. The marginal effects for education and age equal −.040 and −.007; the difference in predicted probabilities for marital status and sex equal −.079 and .014.

For the overall model, the STATA output shows a baseline log likelihood of −300.69 and a model log likelihood (reached after three iterations) of −271.88. Multiplying the difference of −28.81 by −2 gives the chi-square value of 57.63. With four degrees of freedom, the chi-square easily reaches significance.

TABLE 4.2
STATA Probit Analysis Results in Probabilities

Iteration 0: log likelihood = −300.69036
Iteration 1: log likelihood = −272.32072
Iteration 2: log likelihood = −271.87610
Iteration 3: log likelihood = −271.87565

Probit estimates

Number of obs = 510
$\chi(4) = 57.63$
Prob > χ^z = 0.0000

Log likelihood = −271.87565

Pseudo R^2 = 0.0958

Smokes	dF/dx	Std. Err	z	P > |z|	x bar
Education	−.0403348	.0071008	−5.60	0.000	13.1431
Age	−.0065031	.0012264	−5.24	0.000	45.9608
Marital*	−.0790645	.0402579	−1.97	0.049	.545098
Sex*	.0141730	.0400594	0.35	0.724	.552941
Obs. P	.2764706				
Pred. P	.2540010	(at x bar)			

*dF/dx is for discrete change of dummy variable from 0 to 1.

STATA prints a pseudo R^2 of .0958 based on the reduction in the log likelihood (i.e., the chi-square 57.63 divided by -2 times the baseline log likehood). The Aldrich–Nelson measure equals 57.63 divided by 57.63 plus the sample size of 510, or .102. Adjusted upward by taking this value as a proportion of the maximum possible gives a pseudo R^2 of .188. The correlation of the predicted probabilities and observed values of the dependent variable equals .103. By these measures, the variance explained in the probit analysis slightly exceeds the variance explained in the logistic regression.

Summary

Probit analysis deals with the ceiling and floor problems created by a dummy dependent variable with a transformation based on the cumulative standard normal distribution. Despite the familiar nature of the normal curve, the changes in units of the inverse of the cumulative standard normal distribution described by probit coefficients lack intuitive meaning. Further, probit analysis does not allow calculation of the equivalent of odds ratios, and makes calculation of changes in probabilities more difficult than in logistic regression. In most circumstances, researchers will prefer logistic regression, but discussing the alternative logic of probit analysis adds to the more general understanding of strategies of analysis for dummy dependent variables.

5. CONCLUSION

The previous chapters aimed to explain the basic principles underlying logistic regression (and the companion probit analysis) rather than to offer a comprehensive description or mathematical derivation of the techniques for analysis of binary dependent variables. Understanding the basic principles, however, can ease subsequent efforts to master more complex and advanced discussion of logistic regression. Equally important, the basic logic of the logit transformation and maximum likelihood estimation in binary logistic regression applies to a wide variety of other statistical techniques for the analysis of categorical dependent variables. For example, the same interpretations of coefficients for logistic regression with a binary dependent variable fit models with three or more categories of the dependent variable. To emphasize the generality of the underlying principles presented so far, and to offer an introduction to more advanced material, the conclusion briefly reviews the extension of logistic regression to more complex dependent variables

A nominal dependent variable that has three or more categories might lend itself to a set of separate logistic regressions. Three categories might involve three logistic regressions with three dummy dependent variables: the first category versus all others, the second category versus all others, and the third category versus all others. Although the separate logistic regressions would allow for the same interpretations of coefficients as in a single logistic regression, at least three difficulties emerge. First, the separate maximum likelihood estimation for each logistic regression equation ignores overlap across equations. A more efficient method would maximize the joint likelihood for all categories of the dependent variable. Second, when the separate logistic regressions combine two or more categories in making a comparison with one of the categories, they fail to isolate precise contrasts between two categories. More exact comparisons would involve category one versus category two, category one versus category three, and category two versus category three. Third, the use of three logistic regressions for three categories (or four for four categories) contains redundancy. Just as two dummy variables can fully represent three categories of a variable, two logistic regression equations can fully represent relationships of independent variables with three categories of a dependent variable.

Multinomial or polytomous logistic regression (and probit analysis) corrects for these difficulties in analyzing nominal dependent variables with three or more categories, but otherwise does little to change the principles of interpretation used in binary logistic regression. First, multinomial logistic regression jointly maximizes the likelihood that the estimates of the parameters predicting each category of the dependent variable could generate the observed sample data. With only two categories of the dependent variable, multinomial logistic regression estimates reduce to binary logistic regression estimates; the logic of maximum likelihood does not change, only the number of categories increases. Accordingly, the baseline and model log likelihood values, the chi-square statistics, and the pseudo-variance explained measures have similar interpretations in multinomial as in binary logistic regression, except that they apply to models with more than two categories of the dependent variable.

Second, multinomial logistic regression isolates precise contrasts between categories of the dependent variable; and, third, it avoids redundancy by selecting a reference or baseline category. For example, with the last of four categories selected as the baseline, multinomial logistic regression would then estimate sets of coefficients for three contrasts: category one with category four, category two with category four, and category three with category four. Each set of coefficients represents the effects of a unit change in the independent variables on the logged odds of belonging to each category (coded as 1) relative to the reference category (coded as 0). The coefficients are analogous to a binary logistic regression coefficients, but the logged odds refer only to the subset of cases falling into the two categories used in a contrast.

Computer programs for multinomial logistic regression thus present sets of coefficients for each independent variable. Each independent variable affects the logged odds of each category relative to the reference category. The redundancy in all possible contrasts between categories of the dependent variable allows multinomial logistic regression programs to estimate coefficients only for the nonredundant contrasts. Given the specific contrast under consideration, then, the use of odds ratios, partial derivatives, and standardized coefficients discussed in Chapter 2 apply to multinomial logistic regression coefficients.

Understanding logged odds, partial derivatives, and maximum likelihood estimation in binary logistic regression thus provides the tools to understand more complex variations on the analysis of categorical dependent variables. Other variations in forms of logistic regression or probit analysis involve ordinal dependent variables (ordered logit analysis), truncated or censored categorical variables (tobit analysis), and time-dependent categorical variables (event history analysis). More advanced treatments (e.g., Agresti, 1996; Allison, 1984; Liao, 1994; Long, 1997) examine these more complex techniques in depth. Still, the principles of binary logistic regression apply well beyond the topics reviewed in this short volume.

NOTES

1. Nonsensical predicted values are by no means limited to dichotomous dependent variables—unreasonable predictions at the extreme weaken models with continuous dependent variables as well. All such problems warrant attention to the functional form of the relationship.

2. Algebraically, the variance of the error term equals

$$\text{Var}(e_i) = (b_0 + b_1 X_i) * [1 - (b_0 + b_1 X_i)].$$

If the variances are equal for all values of X, they would have no relationship to X. Yet, the equation shows just the opposite—X values influence the size of the error. Taking $b_0 + b_1 X_i$ as P_i, the equation becomes

$$\text{Var}(e_i) = (P_i) * (1 - P_i).$$

As X affects P_i, it affects the error variance, which is greatest when $P_i = .5$, and becomes smaller as P_i deviates from the midpoint.

3. The derivation is

$$O_i = P_i/(1 - P_i),$$
$$P_i = O_i * (1 - P_i),$$
$$P_i = O_i - O_i * P_i,$$
$$P_i + O_i * P_i = O_i,$$
$$P_i(1 + O_i) = O_i,$$
$$P_i = O_i/(1 + O_i).$$

4. The derivation is

$$P_i/(1 - P_i) = e^{b_0 + b_1 X_i},$$
$$P_i = e^{b_0 + b_1 X_i} * (1 - P_i),$$
$$P_i = 1 * (e^{b_0 + b_1 X_i}) - P_i * (e^{b_0 + b_1 X_i}),$$
$$P_i + P_i * (e^{b_0 + b_1 X_i}) = (e^{b_0 + b_1 X_i}),$$
$$P_i * (1 + e^{b_0 + b_1 X_i}) = (e^{b_0 + b_1 X_i}),$$
$$P_i = e^{b_0 + b_1 X_i}/(1 + e^{b_0 + b_1 X_i}).$$

5. Noting that e^{-X} equals $1/e^X$, and that e^X equals $1/e^{-X}$, and letting $b_0 + b_1 X_i$ equal L_i, the derivation is

$$P_i = e^{L_i}/(1 + e^{L_i}),$$
$$P_i = (1/e^{-L_i})/(1 + e^{L_i}/1),$$
$$P_i = (1/e^{-L_i}) * (1/1 + e^{L_i}),$$
$$P_i = 1/[(e^{-L_i}) * (1 + e^{L_i})],$$
$$P_i = 1/(e^{-L_i} + e^{L_i} * e^{-L_i}).$$

Since $e^X * e^Y$ equals e^{X+Y}, and e^{X-X} equals e^0 or 1, the formula reduces to

$$P_i = 1/(e^{-L_i} + 1) = 1/1 + e^{-L_i}.$$

6. Another justification of the logistic regression model and the logit transformation takes a different approach than offered in this chapter. It assumes an underlying, unobserved, or latent continuous dependent variable exists. It then derives the logistic regression model by making assumptions about the shape of the distribution of the underlying, unobserved values and its relationship to the observed values of 0 and 1 for the dependent variable (see, for example, Long, 1997, pp. 40–51). Logistic regression thus describes the relationship of the latent continuous variable to the independent variables.

7. Because of the multiplicative nature of its effects, the actual change in odds depends on the starting point for the odds. The higher the starting odds, the greater the change from the same multiplicative coefficient. For example, a 1.14 increase raises odds of 1 by .14 to 1.14 and odds of 2 by .28 to 2.28. Further, the same multiplicative change in odds will translate into different changes in probabilities depending on the starting point. By describing multiplicative effects, the factor change makes for a simple summary measure, but does not fully overcome the difficulty of interpreting nonlinear relationships.

8. In fact, for logistic coefficients near zero, the logistic coefficient times 100 and the percentage change differ only slightly. Note also that, although the logistic regression coefficients are symmetric around zero, the factor and percentage change in odds do not have this property. The odds, odds ratio coefficients, and percentage change values have no upper bound, but have a lower bound of 0. To compare negative and positive effects on odds, take the inverse. For example, the inverse of an exponentiated coefficient of 2.5 or a 150% increase in the odds equals 1/2.5 or .40, which translates into a 60% decrease.

9. A variation on computing predicted probabilities involves centering the change (Kaufman, 1996). Note that in Figure 2.1, the shape of the logistic curve above the tangent point differs from the shape below that point. In fact, the logistic curve is symmetric only at the midpoint of $P = .5$. With asymmetry, an inconsistency emerges: even when evaluated at the same P, the absolute value of the change in the predicted probabilities for a one-unit increase in X usually does not equal the absolute value of the change in the predicted probabilities for a one-unit decrease in X. The inconsistency does not represent a major problem, as the differences in changes above and below any particular point on the logistic curve are seldom huge, but an alternative calculation avoids the problem. To ensure that the change in the predicted probabilities for a one-unit change in X is identical in either direction, it may be helpful (and not all that difficult) to center the change. As before, calculate the logit for P, but then add half the logistic regression coefficient to the logit and subtract half the logistic regression coefficient from the logit. Calculating the probabilities at these two points and taking the difference still reveals the change in the predicted probabilities for a one-unit change in X, but the change is symmetric around P—an increase or decrease in X gives the same absolute change in the probabilities. In the example for years employed, the logit for P equals 1.586 and the logistic regression coefficient equals .13. The centered change comes from calculating the predicted probabilities and their difference at $1.586 - .065$ and at $1.586 + .065$.

10. Given the difficulty in interpreting standardized dummy variables, some recommend computing standardized coefficients only for continuous variables. However, even if a standard deviation change in a dummy independent variable has little meaning,

standardized coefficients for a dummy variable have value in comparing their influence relative to continuous variables.

11. Calculate the differences in predicted probabilities for a one-unit change in education and age centered around the mean proportion smoking of .276. For education, the logistic regression coefficient divided by 2 equals −.104. Adding that value to the logit of −.964 equals −1.068, and subtracting that value from the mean logit equals −.86. The probabilities associated with logits of −1.068 and −.86 equal .256 and .297. The centered effect of education on probabilities thus equals −.041, which differs only slightly from the uncentered effect. For age, the logistic regression coefficient divided by 2 equals −.017. Adding that value to the logit of −.964 equals −.981, and subtracting that value from the mean logit equals −.947. The probabilities associated with logits of −.981 and −.947 and .273 and .279. The centered effect of education on probabilities thus equals −.006, again only slightly different from the uncentered effect.

12. The maximum likelihood estimate can also be found by setting the derivative of the likelihood function to zero, and solving for the parameter.

13. Using log likelihood values, the formula is $(\ln L0 - \ln L1)/\ln L0$, or, equivalently, $1 - (\ln L1/\ln L0)$.

14. More precisely, it reaches 1 in practice only in the problematic case where the predicted logits explode to infinity and the maximization procedure breaks down (Green, 1993, p. 651).

15. DeMaris (1995, p. 963) shows how to calculate the maximum possible value for the Aldrich and Nelson measure. Dividing the initial measure by the maximum then gives a corrected measure.

16. In SPSS, COMPUTE finds the probability of the cumulative standard normal distribution for any single number or variable using the CDF.NORMAL transformation. With the generate command, STATA uses NORMPROB to find the probability of the cumulative standard normal distribution for a z score. SAS uses the PROBNORM function.

17. To find the z score associated with a probability, SPSS uses COMPUTE with the inverse cumulative distribution transformation called IDF.NORMAL (or PROBIT in early versions of SPSS). STATA uses the INVNORM function, and SAS uses the PROBIT function to do the same.

18. Green (1993 p. 640) indicates that in practice the logit coefficients exceed the probit coefficients by a factor of approximately 1.6.

19. Although the commands in SPSS do not include a function for the density of the normal distribution, the formula can be included directly in the COMPUTE command. SAS also requires direct use of the formula, but STATA has a NORMD function that does the calculation automatically.

APPENDIX: LOGARITHMS

Researchers often find it useful to distinguish between absolute and relative change in a variable. Absolute change ignores the starting level at which a change occurs; in absolute terms, income may increase by $1, $100, or $1000, but the change counts the same at all income levels. Relative change takes a change as a proportion or percentage of the starting level. As a result, the same absolute change counts less at higher starting levels than at lower levels. Using the income example again, a $100 change at $1000 shows a 10.0% increase ((100/1000)*100), whereas a $100 change at $100,000 shows a 0.1% increase. The percentage represents relative change rather than absolute change.

Conversely, the same relative income change results in larger absolute increases at higher levels. Thus, a 10% increase translates into $100 at the starting level of $1000, and into $10,000 at the starting level of $100,000. Depending on the theoretical meaning of a variable, relative or percentage change may prove more appropriate than absolute change in modeling relationships in ordinary regression. It certainly is important in dealing with relationships involving odds in logistic regression.

The Logic of Logarithms

Logarithms offer an effective means of measuring relative change in a variable. The idea behind logarithms is simply to count by multiples rather than by adding ones. Multiples take the form of exponents or powers. For example, using a base of 10, the exponents of 1 to 5 give

$$10^1 = 10,$$
$$10^2 = 100,$$
$$10^3 = 1000,$$
$$10^4 = 10,000,$$
$$10^5 = 100,000.$$

As the power or exponent increases by 1, the resulting value increases by a multiple of 10. The outcome goes from 10 to 100 to 1000 and so on, with each successive value equaling 10 times the previous value. Notice also that a one-unit increase in the exponent or power results in a constant percentage increase in the outcome.

The absolute outcomes increase by values of 90, 900, 9000, and 90,000. However, the percentage increases all equal 9 ∗ 100 or 900% (e.g., $(90/10) * 100 = 900; (900/100) * 100 = 900$). In general, the percentage increase equals the base multiple of 10 minus 1 and times 100.

To define logarithms, let the base equal b, the power or exponent equal n, and the outcome equal X. Then $b^n = X$. Given values of X, logarithms measure the power the base must be raised to produce the X values. They measure the power in the exponent formula rather than X. Therefore, we can define n as the log of X such that $b^{\log X} = X$.

The logarithm of X to the base 10—called a common logarithm—equals the power 10 must be raised to get X. As 10 raised to the second power equals 100, the base 10 log of 100 equals 2. The base 10 log of 1000 equals 3, the base 10 log of 10,000 equals 4, and so on. As before, an increase of one in a logarithm translates into an increase in X by a multiple of 10. An increase of 2 in the log translates into an increase by a multiple of 100 (10 × 10).

In this terminology, X remains in its original absolute units, but the log of X reflects relative or percentage change. As X gets larger, it requires a larger increase to produce a one-unit change in the logarithm. Taking the logarithm thus shrinks values of the original variable above 1, and the shrinkage increases as the values increase. Take the examples in Table A.1.

As X increases by multiples of 10, the log of X increases by 1. As the log of X goes from 1 to 2, X moves from 10 to 100 or increases by 90; as the log of X goes from 2 to 3, X moves from 100 to 1000, or increases by 900; and as X goes from 3 to 4, X moves from 1000 to 10,000, or increases by 9000. Reflecting the nature of percentage change, identical changes in the log of X translate into successively larger increases in X.

TABLE A.1

X	$\log X$
10	1
100	2
1000	3
10,000	4
100,000	5

Following this logic, the same change in X translates into a smaller change in the log of X as X gets larger. A change in X from 10 to 11 implies a change in the log of X from 1 to 1.04. A change in X from 100 to 101 implies a change in the log of X from 2 to 2.004. A change in X from 1000 to 1001 implies a change in X from 3 to 3.0004. Each time X increases by 1, but the log of X increases by successively smaller amounts: .04, then .004, and then .0004. This simply restates the principle that successively larger increases in X are needed to produce the same change in the log of X.

Taking the logarithm of a variable fits the substantive goal of modeling relative change. If the original X measures absolute change, the log of X measures percentage change. In original units, an increase in X of one unit means the same regardless of the initial starting point. In logged units, an increase in X of one unit translates into a larger change at low levels of X than at high levels of X.

Taking the logarithm also has the benefit of pulling in extreme values in a skewed distribution. For many variables, the extreme values lie on the positive or right side of the distribution. To obtain a more normal distribution, and shrink the gap between a few outliers and the rest of the distribution, take the log of such variables. Extremely large values will count less when taking the log of the original variable because of the shift to a percentage scale. In other words, the transformation may place all the cases on a similarly meaningful scale. It does not change the ordering of the cases: the lowest and highest unlogged values remain the lowest and highest logged values, but the relative position and the size of the gaps between the cases change because of the focus on percentage rather than on absolute differences.

Properties of Logarithms

Knowing the value of X, you can find the common logarithm of X on a hand calculator simply by typing in X and then the LOG key. Similarly, knowing the common log of X, you can easily find X by typing in the log value and then 10^X. To solve for a value of X given the logarithm of X, merely treat the log as an exponent. In calculating the values of logarithms and their exponents, note the following properties.

Logarithms are defined only for values of X above 0. No real number exists such that 10 (or any other base) raised to that power produces 0. The same holds for negative values: no real number exists such that

10 (or any other base) raised to that power produces a negative number. A logarithm exists only for numbers above 0. The logarithm of a variable with zero or negative values is undefined for those values. It is necessary to add a constant to the variable so that all values exceed 0 before taking the logarithm.

For values of X between 0 and 1, logarithms are negative. This follows from the logic of exponents. A negative exponent such as in 10^{-2} equals $1/10^2$, 1/100, or .01. Thus, the power that 10 must be raised to produce an X value of .01 is -2. As 10^{-3} equals $1/10^3$, 1/1000, or .001, the log of .001 equals -3. As X becomes smaller and smaller, and approaches 0, the logarithm of X becomes an increasingly large negative number. As X can become infinitely small without reaching zero, the log of X can become an infinitely large negative number. When X reaches 0, the logarithm is undefined.

When X equals 1, the logarithm equals 0 because any number raised to the power 0 equals 1. When X exceeds 1, logarithms produce positive values. As X can increase infinitely, so may the logarithm increase infinitely.

Overall, the X value of 1 and the log X value of 0 define dividing points. Values of X between 0 and 1 produce negative logarithms between 0 and negative infinity; values of X between 1 and positive infinity produce positive logarithms between 0 and positive infinity. Conversely, the larger the absolute value of a negative logarithm (i.e., the farther it falls from zero), the closer the original value comes to zero; the smaller the absolute value of a negative logarithm (i.e., the closer it comes to zero), the closer the original value comes to 1. The smaller the positive value of a logarithm, the closer the original value comes to 1.

Figure A.1(a) illustrates the logarithm function by plotting the common log of X by X. Figure A.1(b) presents the same graph only for values of X up to 20. Negative logarithms show in the graphs for values of X near 0, while positive logarithms show in the graphs for values of X greater than 1. The graphs also illustrate that as X increases, the logarithm changes less per unit change in X. At high levels of X, the curve rises very little: as X takes values ranging from near 0 to 1000, the common log of X rises only to 3. The graphs thus indicate that the logarithm shrinks numbers above 1, with the larger numbers shrinking more than smaller numbers.

The fact that logarithms represent multiples of a base value allows one to translate multiplication into addition of logarithms. Two

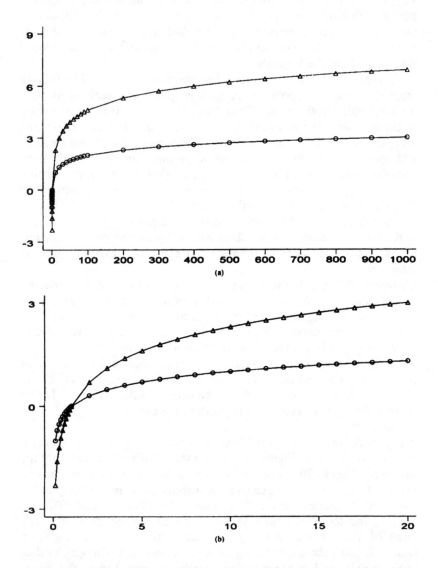

Figure A.1. (a) Common logarithms (open circles) and natural logarithms (open triangles), (b) lower range of common logarithms (open circles) and natural logarithms (open triangles).

properties of logarithms follow. First, the logarithm of a product of two numbers equals the sum of the separate logarithms:

$$\log(X * Y) = \log X + \log Y.$$

For example, the log of (100*1000) equals (log 100)+(log 1000): since the log of 100 = 2, the log of 1000 = 3, and the log of 100,000 = 5, adding the logs gives the same result as logging the product. Second, the log of a quotient of two numbers equals the difference of the separate logs:

$$\log(X/Y) = \log X - \log Y.$$

Thus, the log of (100/1000) equals (log 100) − (log 1000).

Another property proves useful in manipulating equations with logarithms. The logarithm of a power equals the exponent times the log of the base:

$$\log X^k = k * \log X.$$

For example, log 10^5 equals the log of 100,000 or 5; it also equals $5 * \log 10$ or $5 * 1$.

Natural Logarithms

Despite their intuitive appeal, common logarithms find less use than another type of logarithm. Natural logarithms use the base of e, or approximately 2.718, instead of 10. This base has mathematical properties that make it useful in a variety of circumstances relating to computing compound interest, and solving for derivatives and integrals in calculus. Otherwise, however, the logic of logarithms remains the same for e as for 10. The natural logarithm of X (symbolized by $\ln X$) equals the power e must be raised to get X. Natural logs still count by multiples rather than by adding ones, but by multiples of e. The exponents of 1 to 5 of e give

$$e^1 = 2.718,$$
$$e^2 = 7.389,$$
$$e^3 = 20.086,$$
$$e^4 = 54.598,$$
$$e^5 = 148.413.$$

As the power or exponent increases by 1, the resulting values increase by a multiple of 2.718. The exponentials do not increase as quickly as with the base 10, since multiples of 10 exceed multiples of 2.718, but they still increase faster than counting by ones.

To obtain natural logarithms, simply turn this process around. Given X values of 2.718, 7.389, 20.086, 54.598, and 148.413, the natural logs equal 1, 2, 3, 4, and 5. We must raise e by 1 to get 2.718, by 2 to get 7.389, and so on. Typically, X is an integer, so the log of X is not. Let X equal to 5, 27, 62, and 105, to pick some numbers at random. For the first number, 2.718 must be raised to a power between 1 and 2 since 5 falls between 2.718 and 7.389. The exact natural log of 5 equals 1.609. The X value of 27 falls between e raised to the 3 and 4 power. The exact natural log is 3.296. The natural log of 62 is 4.127, and the natural log of 105 is 4.654.

You can obtain the natural log from a calculator simply by typing X and then the LN key. You can verify that, as X gets larger, a one-unit change in X results in increasingly small changes in the natural log of X. As illustrated Table A.2 for values of X greater than or equal to 1, the log of X shrinks the values of X in proportion to their size.

Note that, as for common logs, the natural log is not defined for values of 0 and lower, and that the log of X for values greater than 0 and less than 1 is negative. If a variable has values of 0 or lower, add a constant so that the minimum value exceeds zero before taking the natural log.

The natural log, like the common log, has a straightforward percentage interpretation: a change in one logged unit represents a constant percentage increase in the unlogged variable. To show this, note that to change the log of X back to X, we simply have to raise e to the value of the log of X. For example, on your calculator, type 0, and

TABLE A.2

X	$\ln X$
1	0
2	.693
3	1.099
101	4.615
102	4.625
103	4.635

then the key represented by e^x. The result equals 1. Transforming the log of X into X would show the results in Table A.3.

To see how the natural log of X reflects a constant percentage or relative increase (rather than a constant absolute increase in single units), calculate the percentage change in X for a one-unit change in the log of X. As the log of X changes from 0 to 1, X changes from 1 to 2.718. The percentage change equals

$$\%\Delta = [(2.718 - 1)/1] * 100 = 171.8.$$

For changes in the log of X from 1 to 2 and from 2 to 3, the percentage changes equal

$$\%\Delta = [(7.389 - 2.718)/2.718] * 100 = 171.8,$$

and

$$\%\Delta = [(20.086 - 7.389)/7.389] * 100 = 171.8.$$

In each case, the percentage change equals 2.718−1 times 100. Hence, X changes by the same percentage (171.8) for each unit change in the log of X. An increase of 171.8% is the same as multiplying the starting value by 2.718.

Figures A.1(a) and (b) graph X by the natural log of X along with the common log of X. Compared to the common log of X, the natural log of X reaches higher levels because it takes a larger power to raise 2.718 to X than it takes to raise 10 to X. Overall, however, the shapes of the two curves show important similarities: both show a declining rate of change as X increases.

TABLE A.3

ln X	X
0	1
1	2.718
2	7.389
3	20.086
4	54.598

Summary

Logarithms provide a means to count by multiples. They show the power a base value such a 10 or *e* must be raised to obtain a nonzero positive number. Compared to the original numbers, logarithms rise at a decreasing rate. When numbers greater than or equal to one go up by one, their logs go up by less than one. Moreover, the larger the original number, the smaller the logarithm increases for a one unit increase in the original number. All this makes logarithms appropriate for measuring relative or percentage change rather than absolute change in ordinary regression. It also makes them appropriate for use with the odds of experiencing an event or having a characteristic as modeled in logistic regression.

REFERENCES

AGRESTI, A. (1996). *An introduction to categorical data analysis.* New York: Wiley.

ALDRICH, J. H. & NELSON, F. D. (1984). *Linear, probability, logit, and probit models.* (Sage University Papers Series on Quantitative Applications in the Social Sciences, series no. 07-45). Thousands Oaks, CA: Sage.

ALLISON, P. D. (1984). *Event history analysis: Regression for longitudinal event data.* (Sage University Papers Series on Quantitative Applications in the Social Sciences, series no. 07-046). Thousands Oaks, CA: Sage.

BROWNE, I. (1997). Explaining the Black–White gap in labor force participation among women heading households. *American Sociological Review, 62,* 236–252.

COX, D. R. & SNELL, E. J. (1989). *Analysis of binary data* (2nd ed.). London: Chapman and Hall.

DEMARIS, A. (1990). Interpreting logistic regression results: A critical commentary. *Journal of Marriage and the Family, 52,* 271–277.

DEMARIS, A. (1992). *Logit modeling: Practical applications.* (Sage University Papers Series on Quantitative Applications in the Social Sciences, series no. 07-86). Thousands Oaks, CA: Sage.

DEMARIS, A. (1993). Odds versus probabilities in logit equations: A reply to Roncek. *Social Forces, 71,* 1057–1065.

DEMARIS, A. (1995). A tutorial in logistic regression. *Journal of Marriage and the Family, 57,* 956–968.

ELIASON, S. R. (1993). *Maximum likelihood estimation: Logic and practice.* (Sage University Papers Series on Quantitative Applications in the Social Sciences, series no. 07-096). Newbury Park, CA: Sage.

GREENE, W. H. (1993). *Econometric analysis* (2nd ed.). New York: Macmillan.

HAGLE, T. M. & MITCHELL, G. E., II. (1992). Goodness-of-fit measures for probit and logit. *American Journal of Political Science, 36,* 762–784.

KAUFMAN, R. L. (1996). Comparing effects in dichotomous logistic regression: A variety of standardized coefficients. *Social Science Quarterly, 77,* 90–109.

LIAO, T. F. (1994). *Interpreting probability models: Logit, probit, and other generalized linear models.* (Sage University Papers Series on Quantitative Applications in the Social Sciences, Series no. 07-101). Thousands Oaks, CA: Sage.

LONG, J. S. (1997). *Regression models for categorical and limited dependent variables: analysis and interpretation.* Thousands Oaks, CA: Sage.

MCKELVEY, R. D. & ZAVOINA, W. (1975). A statistical model for the analysis of ordinal level dependent variables. *Journal of Mathematical Sociology, 4,* 103–120.

MENARD, S. (1995). *Applied Logistic Regression Analysis.* (Sage University Papers Series on Quantatitative Applications in the Social Sciences, Series no. 07-106). Thousands Oaks, CA: Sage.

NAGELKERKE, N. J. D. (1991). A note on a general definition of the coefficient of determination. *Biometrika, 78,* 691–692.

PETERSON, T. (1985). A comment on presenting results from logit and probit models. *American Sociological Review, 50,* 130–131.

RAFTERY, A. E. (1995). Bayesian model selection in social research. In (P. V. Marsden, Ed.) *Sociological Methodology 1995* (pp. 111–163). London: Tavistock.

RONCEK, D. W. (1993). When will they ever learn that first derivatives identify the effects of continuous independent variables or "Officer you can't give me a ticket, I wasn't speeding for an entire hour." *Social Forces, 71*, 1067–1078.

ABOUT THE AUTHOR

FRED C. PAMPEL is Professor of Sociology and a Research Associate in the Population Program at the University of Colorado, Boulder. He received a Ph.D. in sociology from the University of Illinois, Champaign-Urbana, in 1977, and has previously taught at the University of Iowa, University of North Carolina, and Florida State University. His research focuses on patterns of demographic change and age-based public policies for the high-income nations during the post-World War II period. Using aggregate data on these nations and years, he has published articles on public spending for children and the elderly, the effects of relative cohort size on fertility and suicide, and sex differences in mortality that have appeared in the *American Sociological Review*, the *American Journal of Sociology*, *Demography*, *Social Forces*, and the *European Sociological Review*. He is currently working on a forthcoming book, tentatively entitled *The Institutional Context of Population Change*.

ACKNOWLEDGMENTS

I thank Scott Menard, Jani Little, Melissa Hardy, Dennis Mileti, Rick Rogers, Scott Eliason, Jane Menken, Tom Mayer, the series editor, Michael Lewis-Beck, and several anonymous reviewers for helpful comments on earlier versions of the manuscript.